MODERN
ROCK AND ICE
CLIMBING

MODERN
ROCK AND ICE
CLIMBING

BILL BIRKETT

A & C BLACK · LONDON

First published 1988 by
A & C Black (Publishers) Ltd
35 Bedford Row, London WC1R 4JH

ISBN 0 7136 5663 8

Birkett, Bill
    Modern rock and ice climbing.
    1. Rock climbing
    I. Title
    796.5'223   GV200.2

    ISBN0-7136-5663-8

Printed in Great Britain by
BAS Printers Limited,
Wallop, Hampshire

CONTENTS

PREFACE

It must be clearly stated that no book or theoretical knowledge alone can make a climber. Competence and sound judgement, the many decisions required by the climber to be effective and safe, require actual experience and mental maturity. Neither can any book be fully comprehensive, covering every individual item of equipment or every nuance of technique. Consequently I have selected the most important components of technique and equipment, explaining their fundamental principles in such a way that only a minimum of improvisation and ingenuity is required to make up the whole. From the sound foundations laid here each individual can fulfil, with the correct experience and training, his or her particular needs and aspirations. Whilst I have written from direct experience, no meaningful work of this nature would be possible without utilising the experienced knowledge of others. If in any way this work appears to stand above others, it is only because I have stood on the shoulders of giants . . . sometimes literally!

ACKNOWLEDGEMENTS

Thanks are due to all my friends with whom I've climbed around the world, particularly the following who have contributed directly with specific advice or help with this book:
John Adams, Stella Adams, Jim Birkett, Mark Chauvin, Paul Cornforth, Frank Davies, Patrick Foott, Rick Graham, Tony Greenbank, Jim Hewing, Andy Hyslop, Julia Laverack, Karen Lewis, Pete Lewis, Tom Nonis, Tim Pavey, Duncan Richards, Dave Rose, Paul Ross, Dave Seddon, Luke Steer, Iain Williamson and John White.

For checking the manuscript I would like to thank:
Rick Graham, Tony Greenbank, Susan Lund and Jon Rigby.

For use of equipment and climbers I would like to thank:
The Climbers Shop – Ambleside, Rock and Run – Ambleside, Europa Sport for Beal rope, Karrimor International, International Mountain School – USA.

Thanks are also due to Paul Renouf of PhotoScope for black and white photograph printing and studio photography.

Note
The photograph on the front of the cover shows Iain Williamson on "Telekenisis" in Pembrokeshire, while the photograph on the back is of Duncan Richards on Great End in the Lake District. (Both photographs by Bill Birkett.)

INTRODUCTION

This book introduces the world of rock and ice and details essential climbing techniques and equipment. It comprises fundamental units which can be used independently or combined to provide a comprehensive overall picture. With due consideration given to the extreme standards in modern climbing and the intense physical and mental preparation necessary, there is separate coverage of both safety and performance.

Rising early from a tent, stiff and white with frost, into the keen, clear air, ready and primed, with the distant objective lit by the rapidly rising sun; total silence broken only by the musical tinkling of ice as it falls away below your crampon points; the warmth of the sun on your back as your fingers play the crystalled granite; the long walk back by the silver light of the moon; the laughter, the loneliness, the challenge; those rare and wonderful days when you feel that nothing is too steep – and it isn't: these experiences and a myriad more are those of the climber and it is from these experiences this book has emerged.

However, romanticism and adventure are not its subjects and, apart from the occasional deviation where I felt a little extra interest would not go amiss, it consists of the pure, basic mechanics of the climbing game. The presentation is straightforward and simple and my objective always is to be as explicit as possible. I make no apologies for this whatsoever, since I feel a book of this nature should inform objectively.

In recent years there has been an incredible increase in climbing standards and a complete metamorphosis in equipment and techniques. Despite this, on my travels around the world it has become increasingly obvious that many climbers do not even understand the basic principles of ropework; for example, whilst some have high climbing ability and the means to purchase high-tech equipment they really do not know how to use it safely. I have also seen that whilst some are proficient in their own specialist fields they are dangerously inept when it comes to performing outside this, e.g. the technical rock climber in a winter mountain situation.

I saw a real need for a book that clearly details the essential requirements of a modern climber and this has been my objective. However, every work must be finite and I am well aware that certain techniques, knots, items of equipment, etc. are not graphically detailed here. My intention has been to cover fully the essential points that are required in the practical climbing situation. Understand this information and it will take only a little ingenuity to devise and work out what else may be required for yourselves.

The mountains give and the mountains take; it is important that the climber understands and can read the environment in which he or she intends to climb. This is the object of the first chapter "Rock and Ice – The Climber's World". There is a lot of information here, the result of long experience in the hills. Understanding it and using it will not only improve your climbing enjoyment but will help you make the right decisions to stay alive.

I thought that all the specialist equipment, which is very different for rock and ice, required detailing and explaining from the beginning, so enabling a full understanding of the techniques that involve this equipment. Accordingly, the second and third chapters discuss rock and ice equipment respectively and have have been written with separate items of equipment detailed as individual units of information. However, for a full understanding of all the techniques involving single and combined items of equipment reference should be sought from the later chapters on techniques. These explain how to use the equipment as a unit in a multi-unit technique.

"Rope Techniques" and "Climbing Techniques" are the fundamental principles involved in all modern rock and ice climbing. The necessary ropework and climbing styles to accomplish a climb in safety are carefully set out here.

"Safety", the penultimate chapter, gives information and advice vital to a climber's well being. The overall philosophy of this book is that a good climber is a safe climber. Climbing is of course many different things to many different people and the last chapter, "Performance", does not forget this important fact.

The essential information is here and I hope it will be of value to those who choose to climb rock and ice. It is important not only to know these facts but also to be able to apply them skilfully and correctly in the practical climbing situation. Practise the knots and techniques and have pride in your climbing craft.

Go in peace and spread the free climbing spirit.

1
ROCK AND ICE –
THE CLIMBER'S WORLD

The reading of the prevailing environment is one of the most fascinating and enjoyable aspects of the climbing game – it is also one of the most important. Accordingly, this chapter examines and defines the climber's world of rock and ice, introducing the various methods and systems of assessment whereby the climber's environment can be appreciated, understood and judged. It is this knowledge, together with the power to interpret accurately, that forms the foundation of sound climbing judgement.

To get the best from your climbing and to keep it as safe as possible you must carefully plan your trip. This holds true even for a day on your local crag and you must be prepared to modify the plan as circumstances and conditions dictate. Set and know your objective and, using sound judgement, give it your best effort.

However, be prepared to return not only when you have achieved your objective but also when it is unsafe to continue. Be prepared to sacrifice an objective however prized. For the good climber safety and success should go hand in hand: it means nought to conquer if you do not live to tell the tale. Enjoy your climbing and be in a position to remember those great days.

STARTING OUT

MENTAL ATTITUDE

I'm afraid if you are smitten with the climbing bug, there is nothing you can do about it. The will to climb is inborn: you can't buy it, it can't be given by others and it cannot be forced upon you; it rises from the heart. So, if it's got you, too, you might as well enjoy it.

To enjoy your climbing to the full it is necessary to climb efficiently and safely. In practice this requires knowledge of a wide variety of techniques and the ability to understand and read the climbing environment.

Whilst this book will increase your knowledge it should be made absolutely clear that the most important ingredient of all in climbing participation, be it bouldering, rock climbing, ice climbing, Alpine mountaineering or expedition work, is the right mental attitude. Without this no amount of knowledge, physical prowess or sophisticated equipment will develop you into a good climber – and a good climber is a safe climber.

FIRST STEPS

It has been said that no inexperienced climber should ever venture out on the hills! This statement, if you think about it, is rather nonsensical. It is true, of course, that experience makes for sound judgement and more rational action, but it is equally true that the only real way to obtain experience is by participation – you have to practise climbing to learn how to do it.

Consequently, the most difficult and dangerous part of any climber's career is often the start. A good way to begin is with friends or family who already have climbing experience. If this option is not available, then to go on a recognised climbing course or with a local guide (this can be inexpensive and can provide invaluable experience) makes good sense. (The necessary information for both these options can be taken from the climbing press or from your local climbing shop.)

There are also a large number of climbing clubs and they occasionally run a meet for beginners. Check your local library for names and addresses. In truth though, most climbing clubs are only useful after you have already gained some experience and have begun climbing.

TYPES OF CLIMBING

Climbing is based on two fundamental elements, which are:

(1) rock climbing and (2) snow/ice climbing.

All the very specialist and different forms of climbing essentially involve, to some degree, one or both of these two basic elements. At this stage it is useful to outline and categorise the main components that make up the climbing world.

BOULDERING — is the purest and most basic form of rock climbing. It involves climbing solo without ropes on rock and boulders up to about 30ft (10m) in height, but generally to a height from where one can jump off without injury. By its very nature it produces rock problems of the highest order of technical difficulty and strenuousness. For some it is an entire sport in its own right; for others it forms an important and pleasurable part of the training programme for rock climbing.

BUILDERING — is much the same as bouldering, but it takes place on buidings or purpose-built climbing walls. It is forming an increasingly important part of rock climbing training programmes because the indoor facilities allow climbing to be undertaken throughout the winter months.

ROCK CLIMBING (FREE CLIMBING OR SPORT CLIMBING) — now takes on a number of different forms but basically it is climbing rock for its own sake — for the pure, simple joy of doing it.

AID/ARTIFICIAL CLIMBING — involves making upward progress by artificial means. This means using anything that is not naturally part of the climb to directly assist progress, i.e. by pulling on inserted nuts, pitons or by using bolts, etc. It is restricted to rock that cannot be free climbed on large walls or overhangs.

BIG WALL CLIMBING — involves climbing rock walls of 1000ft (300m) upwards, generally using a mixture of free and artificial techniques. It is usually a multi-day activity.

SNOW/ICE CLIMBING — involves the use of ice axes and crampons, and varies from easy angled or steeper snow slopes to its purest and most extreme form when climbing vertical or impending ice.

MIXED CLIMBING — involves intermittent snow/ice and rock. It is encountered during Alpine mountaineering and British winter climbing. A recent British trend is to climb hard (summer) rock routes in winter using ice climbing tools.

ALPINE MOUNTAINEERING — is high mountain climbing up a classical mountain feature (ridge, face, etc.) and was traditionally undertaken to reach the summit. Although the climb may be spread over a number of

11

days, with the climbers bivouacking *en route*, the climbers are self-sufficient and undertake the climb in one continous upward push.

EXPEDITION MOUNTAINEERING – is generally a multi-person team climbing in the highest mountain ranges and may include siege tactics (where lead climbers fix ropes and are supported by others carrying supplies and equipment, etc. from below and where they may move up or down the mountain as conditions and logistics dictate) supported by Sherpas and porters. Oxygen and drugs are frequently used to enhance the climbers' performances at altitude.

SOLO CLIMBING – as the phrase suggests, is for the climber who wants to climb alone.

COMPETITION CLIMBING – is widespread in the Eastern European countries and is now spreading to Western Europe and the USA. It can take a number of forms which are judged on speed or technical ability.

THE NATURAL WORLD

Within the basic elements of Rock Climbing and Snow/Ice Climbing there are three major natural factors which alter both the nature and the difficulty of a climb. These are: the crag environment, the prevailing (or imminent) weather conditions, and the type of rock or condition of the ice/snow.

All are interdependent to a certain degree.

ROCK CLIMBING CONSIDERATIONS IN THE CRAG/

MOUNTAIN ENVIRONMENT

The following illustrates a typical mountain rock climbing crag and is labelled with the important physical features that will be referred to in a guidebook or used in climbing conversation.

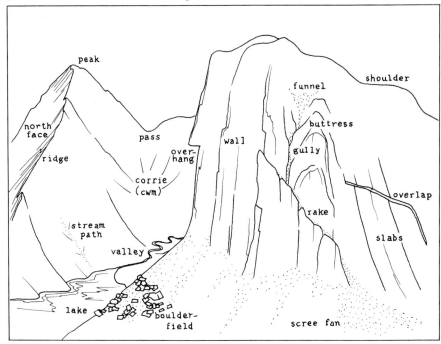

Some important mountain crag features.

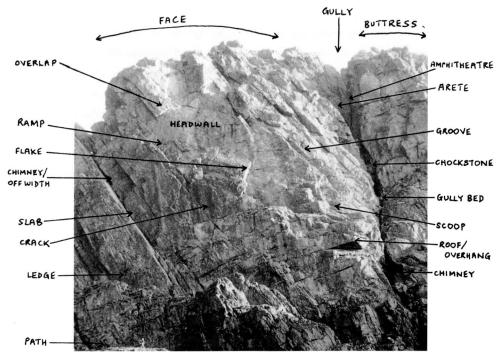

Crag features.

TEMPERATURE CONSIDERATIONS

It is particularly important to study the crag, by reference to the relevant map and guidebook, to determine whether conditions are likely to be suitable for climbing. I refer to this as determining the attitude of the crag. There are two main components: *altitude* and *aspect*, and I will explain their importance.

Observe the *altitude*: the higher it is the colder it will be. For example, during a typical British winter it is impossible to rock climb on Ben Nevis (altitude of crags: 2,000 – 4,000ft (600 – 1200m)), but it may be feasible along the Pembroke sea cliffs (altitude: 0 – 100ft (0 – 30m)).

Observe the *aspect* of the cliff. In the northern hemisphere (Britain, Europe, USA and Japan) the sun rises in the east and sets in the west. It is high in the sky in summer but low in winter because it has moved further south. (I know the earth moves relative to the sun and not vice versa, but this is complicated enough without worrying about that!) A "high sun" means the sun is more directly above and is stronger than when it is "low" and it can touch even northern facing crags at sunrise and sunset. Practically, this means that easterly crags receive the sun in the morning, westerly crags, in the afternoon and evening, and those facing south, for most of the day. North-facing crags will get no sun in winter and generally only around sunrise and sunset in mid-summer.

Examples illustrating these extremes in Britain are: Tremadog and Clogwyn Du'r Arddu. The former, facing south, gets the best of the sunshine all year but the latter (The Black Cliff) does not see the sun at all in winter and only during early morning and late evening around mid-summer. Of course sun means warmth; it dries the rocks quickly and is therefore a critical factor in determining rock-climbing quality.

THE APPROACH

To a certain extent the walk in to a rock-climbing crag will determine the nature of the climbing thereon. A long, arduous walk demanding strength and stamina may lower an individual's climbing ability and due consideration should be paid to this fact. Moonlight or a headtorch often form part of a mountaineer's planning – there is nothing quite like walking back home, after a full day's climbing, in the light of the moon. Consult the guidebook for approach details and bear in mind that as often as not the most direct approach seldom works out to be the quickest.

WATER

If it's going to be hot, you should bear in mind the possibility of obtaining drinking water near or on the crag. Do not drink downstream of any inhabited buildings, drink only running water and watch out for dead animals or other contaminents. If it is obvious that no water can be obtained in the vicinity of the crag, carry some in a light waterbottle.

Expeditions or extended trips into unknown areas should always treat any water with suitable purification tablets or at the very least boil it, and keep it boiling for 10 minutes.

NATURE OF THE CRAG

Each cliff has its own particular characteristics: it may be loose, faulted, vegetated, lichenous, or may present undue rockfall danger. Again, due reference should be made to the guidebook, and the character of the crag established, to avoid disappointment or potential danger. Note any special features and respond accordingly, e.g. in the case of sea cliffs determine to what degree the cliff is affected by the tide. If affected, obtain the current tide times and note the prevailing sea conditions.

INSECTS

During certain months of the year biting insects may make climbing unbearable: Scotland is notorious for the wee midge and the Windy River Range (USA) is noted for the mosquito. This should be checked out carefully to avoid a miserable time. A number of effective repellents are marketed and are well worth the minimal expense.

CLIMBING RESTRICTIONS

Some areas may be restricted during certain times of the year. These include the nesting season for rare mountain birds or colonies of seabirds. This type of ban is usually in effect between the beginning of April and the end of June. Deer stalking in Scotland limits access to a number of estates and this commences, depending on the particular locality, around September for a couple of months. Other bans and restrictions apply to cliffs that are used for military training or to cliffs where climbing would endanger the general public. The Pembroke sea cliffs are subject to military restrictions at certain times and climbing is banned in Cheddar Gorge during the summer tourist season.

In Britain these restrictions, which are detailed in the guidebooks and signposted on the ground, have been painstakingly negotiated on the climber's behalf by the B.M.C. (British Mountaineering Council) and should be strictly complied with. Keeping to these restrictions, in most cases, will preserve our precious natural environment and allow climbers to continue enjoying their present levels of freedom – never take these for granted or abuse the privilege.

WEATHER CONDITIONS

Even for summer rock climbing, especially on mountain crags or large cliffs, a check should be made on the weather forecast. It is posted on notice boards in national parks, and is available through the coastguard for sea cliffs and at guide stations in the Alps. Rain produces slippery rocks and lowers the body temperature. This makes any given rock climb considerably more demanding. Inclement weather can be serious on big walls and care should be taken not to be caught out ill-equipped. Prevailing wind is also an important consideration for determining climbing conditions.

Lightning is another real hazard and if a thunder storm should strike, keep off exposed ridges, etc.

ROCK TYPES

The biggest single factor influencing the nature of any rock-climbing area is probably the type of rock from which the crag is made. It is the rock type, structure and formation which determine the applicable technique.

Geologically the oldest rocks – *sedimentary rocks* – are those made from other rocks. These are formed when erosion products from the mountains are deposited in lakes as sediments and are then compressed and hardened as layer builds upon layer. Sometimes these are again changed due to heat or folding, in which case they become *metamorphic rocks*. The youngest rocks are the igneous rocks and these are formed by molten rock emerging from deep down in the earth's crust and then cooling and hardening. The most spectacular version is, of course, the living volcano.

At this stage it is worth detailing some major, and common, types of rock, introducing their particular characteristics and locating the areas where they can be found.

SEDIMENTARY ROCKS

SANDSTONE – consists of particles of sand cemented together. It varies from soft (Old Red Sandstone – The Old Man Of Hoy) to hard (Torridon Sandstone – The Old Man of Stoer). Depending on the degree of hardness of the rock sandstone gives a combination of strenuous and balance climbing: palming, pulling and mantleshelfing on the sloping holds; friction slabs and strenuous hand jamming in the often flared cracks.

An example of a sedimentary rock is The Old Man of Stoer, a sea stack off the north-west coast of Scotland, which is formed from Torridonian sandstone.

The best protection is by Friends and natural chockstones in the cracks and horizontal breaks. A medium range of Rocks and tapes should also be considered. (In times past wooden wedges or Bongs were used in the cracks.)

Popular sandstone areas: Harrison's Rocks (SW England) – small but popular due to its proximity to London; Helsby (NW England) – small but near Liverpool and Manchester; Northumberland (NE England) – superb small sandstone edges of the finest, rough sandstone scattered throughout the county; and Fontainbleau Forest (N France) near Paris – groups of boulders scattered throughout the forest (Europe's premier bouldering area).

GRITSTONE – is similar in composition to sandstone but is coarser and harder. It gives good friction and balance climbing combined with strenuosness, and climbers often use the small cemented pebbles for their feet or hands. Holds tend to be rounded and palming, pulling and mantleshelving on sloping holds are predominant. However, grit is most noted for its savage, usually flared, hand jamming cracks.

Protection: as for sandstone.

Gritstone occurs most often in the Peak District where Stanage Edge is the longest grit edge and Cratcliffe Tor is one of the highest.

LIMESTONE – is generally white, steep and smooth. It actually consists of compressed marine life, which explains the presence of fossils. It gives steep, strenuous climbing, usually vertical or overhanging. It is necessary to be dynamic and to climb quickly and positively. Good footwork is critical, but the climbing is mainly done with the arms and fingers. It varies in nature and can be alternately loose or sound. In Britain it tends to give flake holds, but elsewhere in Europe the rock is much denser and the only holds available are solution pockets (formed due to the action of rainwater dissolving the rock). Friction is low and, when polished or wet, climbing limestone is akin to climbing a greasy pole.

Protection: can be difficult to secure. A good mixed rack consisting of Friends, Rocks, RP's and tapes for threads and flakes should serve on the more natural (crack) lines in Britain. Elsewhere peg and *in situ* bolt protection is commonplace. Often protection is entirely by bolts (Buoux in France, for example) simply because nothing else would work.

Localities in Britain are numerous, notably in the Peak District (High Tor, Ravenstor and Stoney Middleton) and the sea cliffs of Pembroke. Limestone is predominantly the rock of Europe, and the Verdon Gorge in southern France is one of the world's greatest free rock climbing areas.

METAMORPHIC ROCKS

MICA SCHIST AND GNEISS – is a complex blend of rock types often displaying black and white banding and/or shiny flakes/particles of mica. It varies from rotten to reasonably sound, but has only fair friction and does not readily give positive holds or incuts. It is a difficult rock to read and has holds that are, for the most part, not obvious. It tends to be climbable fairly quickly after rain.

Protection: difficult to get; a mixed rack and quite often pegs can be used.

It is mainly located in Scotland – Creag Dhu at Newtonmore is a large cliff that dries rapidly and is situated just above the road (Cairngorms area). Polldubh cliffs are very accessible and quick-drying crags in Glen Nevis. Strone Ulladale is a massive crag in the Western Isles.

This climb at Compass Point in Cornwall is an example of metamorphic rock (folded mudstone (crimtyphon)).

QUARTZITE – is generally light in colour (it is actually altered sandstone) and is extremely variable as to rock strength and quality. It can feel soapy when damp and provides sharp pinnacle holds (holes that you can put your arm through) and thin flakes resembling biscuits, which demand a certain coolness to use. All holds must be treated with caution.

Protection: a good mixed rack biased to medium size nuts. Rock strength is generally inadequate for the smaller nut placements.

A noted locality is the Gogarth sea cliffs on the Isle of Anglesey.

MUDSTONE/SHALE/SLATE – are changed sediments that have been folded. Often beds of sediments have stood on end leaving smooth (peeling) slabs. A visually extreme example occurs at Sharpnose Point in Devon where vertical bedding planes run out to sea, resembling the thin ribbon blade of a razor. The rock is fundamentally unsound (in varying degrees) and great care and reserve should be exercised by the climber. In the case of quarried slate the rock exhibits a quality known as cleavage and this, in simple terms, means that the rock will split along these lines.

Protection: nut placements are dubious and pegs and bolts are common.

This type of rock is located all round the British coast, notably the Culm Coast in Devon where can be found Blackchurch (horror) and Baggy Point (better). Slate quarries at Llanberis Pass in Wales and Hodge Close in the Lake District are popular.

IGNEOUS ROCKS

GRANITE – is a very hard, compact and coarsely crystalline rock. It forms huge sweeping slabs or vertical cracked faces called exfoliation domes. Friction is superb but the rock is tight (compact) and, depending on the angle, often the only lines of weakness are cracks – often these are up the

17

side of the exfoliating flakes. Depending on the width of the crack, there are a host of techniques which are applicable to granite climbing, from finger jamming to full body bridging.

Protection: mixed rack, dependant on anticipated crack size; some bolt protection on blank faces.

It is located in Cornwall and the Cairngorms. Elsewhere it forms one of the major rock climbing types – the most famous, of course, being Yosemite Valley in the USA. The Black Cuillin in Skye consists of Gabbro which is geologically similar to granite (its frictional properties are legendary).

RHYOLITE – is hard and rough. It displays many different features and is the most commonly climbed rock in the traditional British mountain areas (Wales, the Lake District and western Scotland). The large variety of usually small holds can make this a technically demanding rock on which to climb.

Protection: is equally varied and apart from the very occasional peg runner (*in situ* where required) the art of placing (and removing) runner protection is more highly developed on this type of rock than on any other.

Locations are numerous and include Clogwyn D'ur Arddu, Llanberis Pass, Scafell, Langdale, Borrowdale and Glencoe.

Tumbleweed Connection – rhyolite. An example of igneous rock – Goat Crag in Borrowdale. The photograph shows the nature of climbing on rhyolite.

DOLERITE — is a hard crystalline rock, finer grained than granite but coarser grained than rhyolite. It can offer a full range of good holds, not unlike rhyolite, but generally the friction is even better.

Protection: mixed rack and occasional *in situ* peg.

Locations in Britain include Tremadog and Kilt Rock (Isle of Skye). At Kilt the climbing consists of scaling vertical cracks formed by the hexagonal columnar structure of the rock.

SNOW AND ICE CLIMBING CONDITIONS
IN THE MOUNTAIN ENVIRONMENT

The following illustrates a typical snow/ice climbing environment, with the important physical features named that will be referred to in a guidebook or used in climbing conversation.

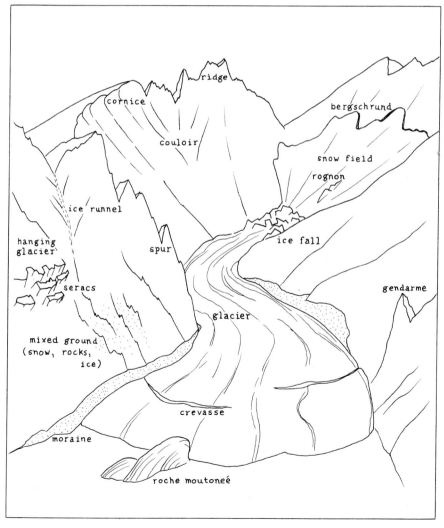

Some snow and ice features in the mountain environment.

TEMPERATURE CONDITIONS

The temperature of the actual chosen climbing locality before and during the planned climb is a major consideration in determining snow and ice condition. Very low temperatures make ice hard but brittle. Temperatures just below freezing give the optimum in ice conditions, and temperatures above freezing make soft slush ice and melt. This will be discussed under "Weather" (see below) and the following observations on temperature are related specifically to the crag locality.

Altitude is an important temperature consideration and, discounting other factors, the higher it is, the colder it will be is the general rule. As a rough guide, in Britain on average every 500ft (150m) increase in altitude lowers the temperature by 1 degree centigrade. Therefore, if on a winter's day it is 0 degrees centigrade in Fort William it could be predicted to be around −9 degrees centrigrade on the summit of Ben Nevis.

The **aspect** of the crag determines sunshine level and this has already been discussed. Suffice to say here that winter climbing on the North Face of the Ben does not require the use of sun cream, whereas a trudge across an Alpine Glacier does!

THE APPROACH

A head torch, map and compass are essential for winter mountaineering, because the daylight hours are at a minimum. To climb entirely in daylight, particularly the longer, remoter and harder mountain climbs, may necessitate a pre-daylight start or, conversely, a descent in the dark. One should always be prepared to climb in the dark with head torch, when things do not go strictly to schedule. Under snow the path disappears and summer features are completely transformed. Additionally, there is always the possibilty of rapidly deteriorating weather and loss of visibility. A map and compass, with the ability to use them, must always be carried on the winter approach. Soft snow, and the associated requirement of breaking the trail, is many times more energy sapping than summer walking and allowance must be made for this in terms of fitness and time. Where possible follow in someone else's footsteps, unless dangerous to do so, as this allows a great saving in strength and energy.

On steep or potentially dangerous ground keep your ice axe where you can instantly get at it in case of a slip or for security. Inevitably, there will be falls on unseen ice. If this happens just relax, tuck your chin onto your chest, and keep your mouth and teeth shut, with your tongue retracted, and retain your hold on the ice axe.

Beware of flat plains of snow in hollows or valley bottoms where water may lay below. Snow disguises very thin ice and to break through and get wet in cold conditions can often prove fatal.

Always be on the look out for potential avalanche danger.

WEATHER – Weather is air/moisture movement and this controls wind, temperature, precipitation (rain, snow or hail) and visibility. Naturally, it is critical in determining snow/ice conditions; it can bring sunshine or storm, good climbing conditions or potential disaster. Every single time one ventures out onto the hills in winter it is essential to know the weather forecast and to be prepared accordingly. This includes deciding to stay off the hills in extreme conditions.

Weather is a complex subject and there are a number of books concerning mountain weather interpretation. However, its prediction is best done by experts and their satellites. Up-to-date area information should be obtained and, apart from the sources indicated previously, there is usually a telephone weather information service in mountain areas.

Some weather-related considerations should be studied carefully by the climber.

Temperature determines snow and ice conditions and the form of precipitation (rain, hail or snow). Both these factors are controlled by the wind and the chilling effect of this cold wind on the human body is known as Windchill. In any wind, but particularly in winds with speeds up to 15 m.p.h. (24 k.p.h.), the chilling effect reduces the body heat to a much lower degree than the cooling produced by temperature alone (this is strange but true). For example, an air temperature of +5 degrees centigrade with a wind of 50 m.p.h. (80 k.p.h.) gives an equivalent still air cooling effect on the body of −12 degrees centigrade. Obviously windchill can be a severe hazard and the mountaineer should have adequate windproof clothing to resist it.

Rainfall and melt produce severe avalanche conditions.

Snowfall can take a myriad different forms. The safest rule for the mountaineer is to stay off the hills whilst it is snowing and for a minimum of 24 hours afterwards. Fresh snow is unconsolidated; it can't be climbed, it makes walking exhausting, it obscures visibility, it 'wets' the climber—lowering the body temperature, and and it avalanches. The rate of snowfall is an important consideration in determining avalanche potential.

Strong wind and snow means blizzard conditions. Blizzards repeatedly kill mountaineers. A true blizzard experience cannot adequately be described in words; it is ferocious, unforgiving and frightening. Visibility is reduced to virtually zero; often you cannot see your feet — a total whiteness blanks out all perspective and frames of reference. Snow shifts and accumulates into large drifts; it is a world on the move. The windchill becomes intense, your body being the only resistance to the continuous wave of wind and cold. Snow penetrates even the most appropriate clothing and survival in these conditions is a difficult and strategic battle.

SNOW AND ICE CONDITIONS

The understanding and reading of the prevailing physical conditions directly dictate the ice-climbing day. It is a wide subject with complex inter-relationships and full appreciation can only be gained when theoretical knowledge is combined with actual experience.

Do not have prefixed rigid plans, for you must always react to the prevailing conditions. This will give you the satisfaction of the best climb possible on the day and, more importantly, help you survive. The following information defines the basic fundamentals.

Though both snow and ice may be only frozen water, there are many different forms and metamorphisms that radically affect the climbing quality. Remember that very low temperatures make ice hard and brittle, temperatures just below freezing give the optimum climbing conditions, and temperatures rising above freezing make for soft slushy ice (if caught early enough this makes for the technically easiest form of ice climbing, but this condition is fraught with obvious danger).

Another extremely important observation is that snow and ice require time to "mature" (to build up sufficiently and to come into good climbable condition) before safe and satisfactory climbing can be had.

In Britain the snow and ice climbing vary tremendously, with the most persistent and reliable conditions to be found the further north one travels. Although both Wales and the Lake District can have magnificent winter climbing conditions, the duration tends to be short. Scotland is the most consistent winter climbing ground in Britain. However, suitable winter climbing conditions can *never* be guaranteed. For example, the classic hard ice climb on Ben Nevis, Point Five Gully, has been known to be in condition in a poor winter for literally only a few days or, conversely, in a good season it has been climbed (in true winter conditions) over a time span of seven months (from November to May in the winter of 1985/86)!

SEASONS

On average, in Britain January, February and March are the most reliable months. February can be best when there has been an early build up of ice and snow which has had time to mature. However, it may be that February deposits fresh snow and remains cold, resulting in conditions where spindrift and brittle ice predominate. Possibly March will give better conditions; certainly the daylight hours will be longer. There are no hard and fast rules. One must simply observe the conditions and take note. If you wish to visit an area it is worth contacting the climbing shop local to the area, or a resident climber – a quick phone call is sound practice.

In the USA ice climbing in New Hampshire is usually in condition between late November and late March. In Colorado the season tends to be a little shorter.

In the European Alps the official winter climbing season lies between December 21st and March 21st. (Unlike Britain, snow and ice remain in the mountains throughout the year.)

The following is a summary of the fundamental snow and ice conditions:

FRESH SNOW – is soft and useless to climb. It makes for difficult walking on easy angled ground and avalanche conditions on steeper ground. Stay off the hills/mountains whilst it is snowing and for an absolute minimum period of 24 hours after snowfall.

BLOWN SNOW – is the airborne movement of fresh or unconsolidated snow. If the temperature is relatively high it may be wet and clammy. This phenomenon is the building process for snow/ice climbing conditions. It builds cornices, fills gullies and plasters the rock buttresses. In its early stages it brings acute avalanche danger.

POWDER SNOW – is fallen snow that, due to temperatures constantly below freezing, remains as a light, fluffy, unconsolidated and potentially mobile mass.

HAILSTONE – can fall for a period of time sufficient to form a, generally, non-cohesive layer of "ball bearings". Often it is subsequently covered by snow and this forms a plain of weakness and hence an unstable snow mass.

CRUSTED SNOW (*SEE* WIND SLAB) — occurs when only the surface of the snow hardens but the mass underneath remains soft. It can occur in two ways:
(i) by the sun melting the surface of the snow and this subsequently re-freezing into a hard crust, or
(ii) due to an icy wind freezing only the surface of the snow mass.
   The crust may overlay powder snow or snow that is still soft and unconsolidated. On easy slopes this makes walking exhausting — you take a step which partially supports your weight, then in mid stride the crust breaks and you sink into deep snow. On steeper slopes crusted snow makes for avalanche danger.

SPINDRIFT — is blown/mobile powder snow. It collects in large drifts, builds cornices and collects on ledges and easy angled slopes. Because it is incohesive it builds up where it is deposited, in the lee of the wind, until its mass becomes too heavy to be self-supportive and it collapses and avalanches. Typical temporary holding localities include basins, the easier angled sections of faces, ledges and the narrow confines at the tops of gullies. Spindrift avalanches are common (particularly early in the Scottish winter climbing season) and are a perpetual nuisance, especially for the gully climber. (Hanging on through them tends to be uncomfortable rather than fatal.)

WIND SLAB — occurs when only the surface is wind/cold hardened but the mass remains unconsolidated. The stabilising factor is only the strength of the crust and, on steeper slopes when this is broken (by a trail of footsteps punching through the hard skin or by the run of a ski), it is likely to avalanche.
   When walking on the tops of mountains a sure sign of windslab/powder down in the gullies/couloirs below is the presence of raised footsteps. These appear when soft/powder snow is first consolidated by the weight of a person stomping it down and making it hard; the snow compressed by the foot remains standing proud and the surrounding soft powder is blown away to be deposited below. A check on the direction of the wind that prevailed to cause this and therefore the point at which the deposited (and avalanche prone) unconsolidated snow is likely to lay can be effectively made by examining the footstep to check in which direction the Rime Ice (for definition of Rime Ice see below) has formed. Rime Ice grows its fingers into the wind; therefore, it is the opposite side where the deposited snow may be found.

CONSOLIDATED SNOW — occurs to lain snow after a period of time (absolute minimum period after snowfall is 24 hours but 3–7 days is more realistic, depending on the prevailing conditions) and is formed when the individual snow crystals begin to reform and interlock. This may be due to alternate melting and re-freezing or due to the effects of pressure from further snow being laid above.

NÉVÉ — is the best climbing snow, where the climber's axes and crampons penetrate without undue difficulty but hold solid. It is tough and reliable. One distinguishing feature of névé is the wonderful squeaking noise heard when placing and removing the crampon points. It is produced from snow that has melted and re-frozen to a sufficient degree to form an optimum density.

OLD SNOW — after melting and re-freezing and consolidating a number of times the crystal structure of the snow changes significantly to become extremely hard (Black Ice/Snow) or alternatively it degenerates to become rotten or hollow (Sugar Snow).

AERATED SNOW/SNOW MUSHROOMS – a suitable combination of extremely low temperatures and wind-blast produces snow mushrooms on ridges and summits. Additionally, large snow faces may be fluted with ridges of aerated snow. These are notable features in Patagonia and Alaska. Both are hollow and unsupportive and the climber is required to plunge in axe and arm to full depth in order to make progress. The adopted technique is best described as swimming.

RIME ICE – is essentially frost fingers that point in the direction of the wind that formed them. They are created by supercooled droplets of water from the atmosphere freezing on an exposed surface. Occasionally they are strong enough to climb upon. They serve as a useful pointer to determine wind direction and hence to deduce the location of unconsolidated blown snow (possible avalanche danger).

HOARFROST – occurs when water vapour from the atmosphere sublimates onto a surface; this can be rock, tree or climber.

VERGLAS – this is a thin transparent layer of ice that shrouds the rocks. It makes for hard climbing conditions because it effectively prevents the use of rock holds and is usually too thin to support an axe or the front points of crampons on steep ground. It necessitates the use of crampons. It can be formed under a number of different weather conditions: freezing of rain onto the rock, wet rocks that are subsequently subjected to freezing, or freezing fog.

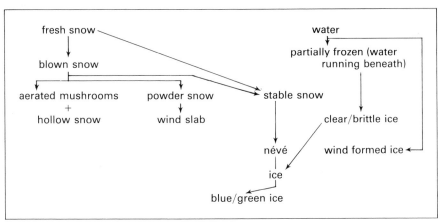

The basic elements and their inter-relationships in the formation of snow and ice.

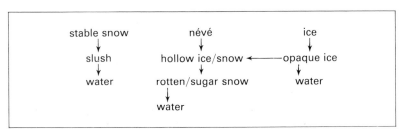

The deterioration sequence.

WATER ICE — when new this is usually clear (unless the water bears mineral salts and is already coloured) and is brittle; often in this state it shatters on placement of axe and crampon front points. In later stages the ice becomes tougher (stronger) and this type of ice (frozen waterfalls) gives the main type of climbing in many areas of the world.

ICE FROM SNOW — this is the best category of ice for climbing and is usually the most prevalent on the British hills. It takes many forms and a good indication of the type and its climbing quality is its colour: a grey colour indicates unsound, hollow or thin ice; transparent ice indicates newly formed ice and is brittle; blue/green ice is the very best ice on which to climb and place ice screws; black ice is derived from old and compressed snow and is usually found in the avalanche/wind-polished areas of couloirs or snow basins. It can be rock hard and makes for difficult and tiring placement of axe and crampons.

USING GUIDEBOOKS

For each major climbing area there exists a climber's guidebook. These books are essential reading for the keen climber, because they guide you to an area, a crag and the climb of your particular choice. They also describe accurately and in detail the route taken by the climb you wish to follow. Used fully and correctly a guidebook plays a major role in a successful and safe climbing day.

TYPES OF GUIDEBOOK

There are a number of different types of guidebook:

(1) The definitive guidebook covers in detail one particular climbing location within a major climbing area and attempts to include (locate, describe and grade for difficulty) all the climbs that exist in that area. These are usually prepared by the leading climbing clubs of the area or, for instance, the British Mountaineeering Council. An example of such a guidebook would be *Borrowdale* by the Fell and Rock Climbing Club of the Lake District, which covers exclusively rock climbing in the Borrowdale valley. This club's series of guidebooks covers the whole of the Lake District, splitting it geographically into its major climbing grounds.

(2) The selected climbs guide covers only the best routes in any one major area. An example would be *Rock Climbing In The Lake District* by Birkett, Cram, Eilbeck and Roper, published by Constable.

(3) The winter climbing guide covers one major area. An example would be *Winter Climbs In The Lake District* by Bennett and Birkett, published by Cicerone Press.

It helps to understand quickly how a guidebook is structured. When a climber takes a line that has never to his knowledge been climbed before, and it is a good one worthy of being climbed by others, he records the fact in a "new routes book" which may be kept in a climber's shop or a local pub or climbing hut. From here the description can be copied by others who may wish to tackle the route or, ultimately, by the guide-writers or those who report the climbing news for the climbing press.

The route description follows a carefully defined formula which has been developed over the years. It tells you the area in which the climb lies, the crag and its position on the crag, and then it gives the name, grade and length of the route, breaking it into convenient rope lengths (pitches).

An example of a British route description would be as follows:

THE AREA

THE CRAG

THE TOTAL LENGTH OF THE CLIMB

Borrowdale, Lower Falcon Crag

STAR INDICATES THE RELATIVE QUALITY OF THE ROUTE

*Star Wars 170ft E3

THE OVERALL GRADE OF DIFFICULTY

A steep route, requiring bold climbing, over the bulges below and above the obvious niche in the centre of the crag. Start by a slim groove in the bulging grey wall,

PITCH LENGTH beside a small hawthorn bush.

PITCH NUMBER (THIS IS THE FIRST PITCH...

(1) 70ft (5c) Climb directly to a bulge. Step left and climb through the bulge, on the right side of the niche, using a hollow flake with care! Belay at the back of the niche.

THE TECHNICAL GRADE

... AND THIS IS THE SECOND PITCH)

(2) 100ft (5b) Up the back of the niche (peg runner) and then traverse right to the nose. Pull straight over the bulge, past a peg runner, to a groove. Climb the groove slightly leftwards to finish up a short crack/slab, 15 left of the top pitch of The Niche.

FA 8th April 1978 B Birkett, R Graham (alt).

SHOWS THE ROUTE WAS FIRST ASCENDED ON THIS DATE BY THE NAMED CLIMBERS.

INDICATES THAT BIRKETT & GRAHAM ALTERNATED THE LEAD, BIRKETT LEADING THE FIRST PITCH AND GRAHAM THE SECOND.

(Shared) FOLLOWING THE NAMES INDICATES THAT THE LEAD WAS CHANGED OVER UNTIL ONE OF THE CLIMBERS SUCCESSFULLY LED THE PITCH. IT CAN ALSO MEAN, ON A MULTI-PITCH ROUTE, THAT THE NAMED FIRST ASCENSIONISTS HAVE EACH LED CERTAIN PITCHES, BUT NOT NECESSARILY ALTERNATELY. WHEN THIS IS THE CASE IT IS USUAL TO INDICATE THE ACTUAL PITCHES LED BY SHOWING THE PITCH NUMBER IN BRACKETS AFTER THE NAME, E.G.

F.A. Jo Bloggs (1,3 & 4), Fred Smith (2) - SHOWS SMITH LED ONLY PITCH 2 OF A FOUR-PITCH ROUTE.

IF ONLY NAMES ARE GIVEN, IT MEANS THAT ONLY THE FIRST NAMED LED AND THE OTHER NAMED CLIMBERS FOLLOWED.

A typical description to be found in a guidebook.

In addition to the worded description, there is usually a sketch or photograph delineating the line of the route to be taken. Often this is the best way actually to pick out the line and direction of a climb.

Note that for longer rock climbs in, for example, Verdon or Yosemite the description may be given in a stylised sketch with symbols representing the different features. This is known as a "Topo" and each area has its own set of symbols which are translated by buying the local guidebook.

(Opposite)

This typical Topo illustrates a rock climbing route in a mountain setting. The grade is an overall French/Alpine grade but the hardest technical difficulty is shown for each pitch. The features of the route should be carefully noted, particularly pitch 4 whose technical grade is 7b and which is considerably harder than the rest of the climb. Below this hard section lay an overhang and a large cave, so retreat may well be extremely difficult. Also, observe that although the descent is technically easy (no abseiling), there are some large, loose boulders present above the glacier/snow field, so due care should be taken.

Topos differ for each area, but they are all devised in such a manner as to be clearly understood. The key to the symbols, and the different grading system, must be looked at first. Then the Topo must be carefully studied before any climb is attempted.

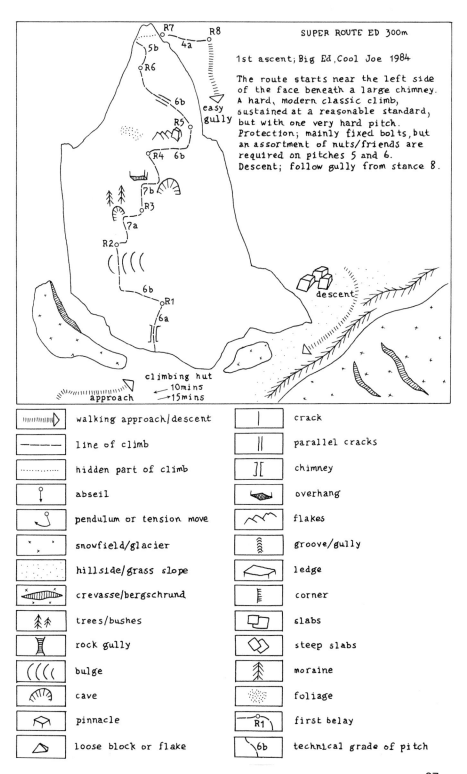

SUPER ROUTE ED 300m

1st ascent; Big Ed, Cool Joe 1984

The route starts near the left side of the face beneath a large chimney. A hard, modern classic climb, sustained at a reasonable standard, but with one very hard pitch. Protection; mainly fixed bolts, but an assortment of nuts/friends are required on pitches 5 and 6. Descent; follow gully from stance 8.

⑉⑉⑉▷	walking approach/descent	│	crack
─ ─ ─	line of climb	‖	parallel cracks
··········	hidden part of climb	][	chimney
♀	abseil	⌒	overhang
⌡	pendulum or tension move	⌃⌃	flakes
ˣ ˣ	snowfield/glacier	≋	groove/gully
∴∴∴	hillside/grass slope	⬠	ledge
⬛	crevasse/bergschrund	⌷	corner
⅄⅄	trees/bushes	⬓	slabs
⊟	rock gully	⬦	steep slabs
(((	bulge	⅄	moraine
⌒	cave	∴∴	foliage
⬠	pinnacle	R1	first belay
△	loose block or flake	⟍6b	technical grade of pitch

27

GETTING THE BEST FROM A GUIDEBOOK

There is a lot of information in a good guidebook, although it will be noted that it is presented in a concise and factual manner. It is up to the individual to make the most of this information and, much like learning a foreign language, interpretation is required to make good sense of it.

What a guidebook can do is help you to select an area, a crag and a climb that will provide you with a good day out, whatever the prevailing conditions (there are some exceptions) and at any time of the year.

It is important to determine the *attitude* of a climb. This term refers to the position of a climb: its geographical location, its height above sea level, the direction in which it faces and its physical properties (i.e. type of rock – it could be vegetated and loose, or clean and quick drying). By determining the altitude of a climb and the direction in which it faces and combining this information with the seasonal climatic conditions it is possible to select a route to suit prevailing conditions.

Although most guidebooks don't give you this information directly, the essential component parts are usually there and with use of a map one can quickly determine the attitude of any particular climb. The following points and common sense decisions (e.g. keeping away from easily accessible crags and climbs only a short walk away from the road and avoiding public holidays when crags will inevitably be crowded) will guide you towards a successul climbing day.

A south facing crag gets the sunshine throughout the day, one facing east will only receive it in the morning and one facing west will get the sunshine in the afternoon. One facing north may never get the sun (depending on the time of year) and consequently may remain cold all day.

The higher the cliff above sea level, the colder the air temperature. If you are looking for early ice climbing, then this is important but, for example, if you are wanting to rock climb, then high north-facing crags should be avoided early in the season.

For Britain the climatic divisions are reasonably clearly defined within their geographical locations and these are worth noting. Generally, the SOUTH-WEST is the mildest and warmest area of the country and the granite Cornish sea cliffs usually provide rock climbing for twelve months of the year. In summer, on the south-facing cliffs, it may well be too hot to climb until evening. There is no noted winter climbing.

WALES – is a traditional mountain climbing area and in the mountains it is usual to rock climb between April and October. Winter climbing, with reasonable snow and ice climbing conditions, can usually be had between the end of December and February. However, there are a number of sea cliffs and low lying crags for year round rock climbing, notably those of Pembroke, Anglesey and Pen Trwyn at Llandudno.

THE LAKE DISTRICT – the wettest region of England, is another traditional mountain climbing area and rock climbing is usually reserved for the months between April and October. Winter climbing is the most reliable between December and March.

SCOTLAND – is a vast upland mountain area and is the most hostile, the most northerly and the coldest of the British climbing areas. The east coast (Cairngorms) is usually drier than the west (Glencoe), but it is consistently the coldest area. It is often possible to rock climb between May and September but be prepared for the Scottish midge. The winter climbing season is the longest and most reliable in Britain and can stretch through December and March.

Other information which is often presented in guidebooks, and must be carefully observed, is that of *Climbing Restrictions*. These may operate at certain times of year or on certain sections of a crag. Typically, they are a voluntary agreement to preserve important bird nesting or rare plant sites, although sites of Special Scientific Interest (SSIs) are protected by law and heavy fines will result if the restrictions are ignored. The restrictions are usually the result of protracted and difficult negotiation by the British Mountaineering Council with landowners and other concerned bodies, and they should be strictly observed. Failure to observe restrictions not only will destroy the beautiful natural environment but will lead to a total ban on climbing activity.

A natural restriction on sea cliffs is, of course, the tide and this should not be forgotten. Tide times and cycles fluctuate throughout the year and so this information cannot be given in a guidebook – but in the guide you will find the address/telephone number from where the current information can be obtained. Check tide times carefully and note that tides can rise by some 30ft (9m) (low to high).

Once the above information has been considered and you have decided on the area and best cliff to climb upon for the time of year, bearing in mind the prevailing conditions, the choice of route must be made. Most guides include a *Star System* as an indication of quality and this, of course, will help the decision, but the most important single factor must be your own judgement. In the critical decision, the difficulty of the climb must be one of the most significant factors and the following information on grading the difficulty of a particular climb is important.

DETERMINING THE DEGREE
OF DIFFICULTY OF A CLIMB

All established climbs are graded according to their degree of difficulty. By this means a climber can select a route to suit his requirements on any particular day. The guidebook system of grading climbs is remarkably good and is now generally consistent throughout the climbing regions. Of course there are local variations and a trend to undergrade an area's particular specialities – you should be aware of this.

However, the grading of climbs is a subject that over the ages has caused more (friendly) argument than any other; it will always be so because of the many variables involved. To illustrate this we can turn to rock climbing.

Any rock climb will be different for each individual climber. It may be easier for a tall man with a long reach or, conversely, the climbing may involve a sequence of moves through overhanging rock where the disposition of the holds favours the climber of smaller stature. Even if two climbers are of equal stature each may favour and be better at different styles of climbing: a climb may be desperately strenuous, favouring the climber with strong muscles, or perilously delicate, favouring the climber with a cool head.

Additionally, the prevailing conditions markedly affect the grade of a climb; on a hot, sweaty day a friction climb becomes hard but a north-facing crack will seem much friendlier than on a colder day.

So, you can see that the difficulty of any single climb varies with:
(a) the physical characteristics of the climber;
(b) the climber's particular ability to use specific techniques;
(c) the prevailing physical conditions.

However, carefully note that climbs are given only one grade, although this may comprise a number of component parts. Clearly, also, the grading of snow and ice climbing becomes even more difficult because the physical conditions, the build up of snow and ice, vary so much. Almost on a daily basis a winter climb can vary from a hard struggle to an easy plod.

Considering all the above factors, the grading of difficulty given in guidebooks is remarkably accurate and it is up to the individual to assess the variables, both by knowing his/her own abilities and by carefully assessing the prevailing conditions. To achieve this degree of accuracy the grading system is by necessity of some sophistication.

BRITISH GRADING SYSTEM

In Britain there are two systems used together to grade (free) rock climbs, and there is a further separate system of grading winter climbing. Other countries have entirely different systems of grading. To explain each different system would be extremely space-consuming, so I will give a simple table of comparison, using the British system as the standard reference. (See the diagram below.)

Used Together		
British Overall Grade		British Technical Grade
Moderate		1a
Difficult		2a
Very Difficult		2b
Severe (Mild)		2c, 3a
Severe		3a, 3b
Severe (Hard)		3b, 3c
Very Severe (Mild)		4a, 4b
Very Severe		4b, 4c
Very Severe (Hard)		4c, 5a
Extremely severe	E1	5a, 5b
	E2	5b, 5c
	E3	5c, 6a
	E4	6a, 6b
	E5	6a, 6b
	E6	6b, 6c
	E7	6c, 7a

British rock climbing grades. Notice that there is an *Overall* system of grading and this is used in conjunction with a *Technical Grade*.

ROCK CLIMBING GRADES

The Overall system begins with "Moderate" and proceeds up to "E7" (Extremely Severe 7th grade), although it should be noted that this is an open-ended system and expands as routes of greater difficulty are climbed – at the time of writing a number of E8's and an E9 have been claimed but have not yet been included in any guidebook. The Overall grade takes into account the overall difficulty, strenuosity, position and seriousness of a climb, and the resultant impression of all these functions gives the grade. Really, it is based on experience of many climbs and is relative from one climb to another.

In addition to this Overall grade, there is a Technical (numerical/alphabetical) grade which relates to the hardest single move on any particular section (pitch) of the climb. Although the Technical grade, theoretically, begins at "Moderate " difficulty (1a), in practice it is usually only used for climbs of Overall grade "Very Severe" and above.

It can be seen that the numerical part of the technical grade was conceived to represent one particular category of the overall grade and the alphabetical part (a, b, and c) represents increased technical difficulty within that particular Overall grade:

i.e. "Very Severe" can be 4a, 4b or 4c.

However, the system occasionally extends beyond the above confines and, for example, the technical grade of the hardest move on a route may well be 5b but the Overall Grade could be Hard Very Severe, E1 or E2. The route would only be given Hard Very Severe in exceptional circumstances, perhaps where the hard move was actually leaving the ground and where the rest of the route did not exceed a technical grade of 5a. Generally, the route would get E1 if there was only a short section of 5b climbing, but it could be given E2 if the difficulties were sustained or the 5b section was a long way from any protection.

So much for the theory, but really the only way to understand fully the British grading system is to experience the climbs for yourself: then at least you can enter the arguments with some conviction!

Britain	France	UIAA	USA	Australia
4a	4+V	V	5.6	15
4b	5	V+	5.7	16
4c	5	VI	5.8	17
5a	5+	VI	5.9	18
		VI+		
5b	6a	VII	5.10a	19
			5.10b	20
5c	6b	VII	5.10c	21
			5.10d	
		VII+		
6a	6c	VIII	5.11a	22
			5.11b	23
6b	7a	VIII	5.11c	24
		VIII+	5.11d	25
6c	7b	IX	5.12a	26
				27
7a	7c	IX	5.12b	
		IX+	5.12c	28
			5.12d	
	8a	X	5.13a	

Table comparing International grading systems.

THE IMPORTANCE OF THE GRADING OF ROCK CLIMBS

The reason behind the apparently complicated grading system lies partly in its historical background and partly in the diverse nature of British rock climbing. Despite all, it is a system that works very well, although to those beginning the sport the wide range of grades may be difficult to comprehend. How can there be so many different grades? Indeed, when you climb at your best and begin to attempt increasingly difficult routes there are really only two grades – those climbs you can do and those you can't!

However, for most intermediate stages in your climbing career, or when visiting a climbing area for the first time, knowing the grades of the rock climbs is essential to a full, enjoyable and safe day on the rocks. The present day wide range of difficulty has arisen mainly because of the vast improvement in climbing equipment and techniques. Owen Glynne Jones, a pioneer of his day, created routes of Very Severe standard before the turn of the century and Jim Birkett pioneered E1 (Extremely Severe) in the 1940s. Although Birkett's equipment was better than that of Jones, both had an absolute minimum of protection in the event of a leader fall. The old adage was simply that you should never fall off, for it would most likely prove fatal. In those days it was the mental barrier that was the biggest single factor in establishing the grade that could be safely climbed.

Since those early days equipment, friction footwear, protection and training techniques have steadily advanced to their present level of sophistication. With them has advanced the standard of pure technical difficulty. Accordingly, a few comments on particular grades of difficulty are relevant and will give a clearer understanding of what each different grade represents.

MODERATE – this gives a technically simple climb, involving use of hands as well as feet, which is a little more than a scramble. However, the rock may not be of the best quality and although technically easy it may follow a line of weakness up a large face of rock and present considerable exposure. It most definitely is a climb.

Example: "Crescent Climb" on Pavey Ark in the Lake District.

VERY DIFFFICULT – a climb with some technicality and including steep rock. Often the consequences of a leader falling, even with modern protection, could be disastrous due to the likelihood of hitting the rocks below during a fall. (On steeper, technically harder routes in the extreme category a leader fall with correctly placed protection can be completely safe.) There is a great deal of adventure in climbing at this grade and it gives some fine natural routes up large cliffs. Although many beginners have their teeth cut on a "Very Difficult", experienced climbers will lower their standard to climb at this level of difficulty in wet conditions.

Examples: "Bosigran Ridge" at Bosigran in Cornwall, "Outside Edge Route" on Craig Yr Ogof (Cwm Silyn) in North Wales, "Little Chamonix" on Shepherds Crag in the Lake District.

VERY SEVERE – for many years this was the hardest grade given to any climb in Britain. (It was the case in Scotland almost into the 1980s – even though there existed climbs that are now recognised to be E3!) This is the grade where most climbers begin to observe the pure Technical grade (4a, 4b, 4c) alongside the Overall grade. It is a standard at which a fit and proficient climber of average ability can make some magnificent rock climbs.

Examples: "Direct Route" on Dinas Mot, in Llanberis Pass, North Wales, "Overhanging Bastion" on Castle Rock in the Lake Distict, "The Old Man Of Stoer", a sea stack off north-west Scotland.

E1 (5A) TO E2 (5B) – extremely hard rock climbs requiring a high degree of ability, commitment, fitness and strength. A sound awareness of, and ability to use, modern equipment is needed to safeguard this kind of climbing standard. Nevertheless, many rock climbers of good natural ability and with developed skill in the use of modern techniques and equipment can achieve this standard. (The late Bill Peascod climbed E1 with me when he was well into his sixties.) After this grade is obtained it really is up to individuals to form their own opinions as they discover the intense thrill of extreme climbing. Routes of recognised quality within the E1/E2 grades include:

"Coronation Street" E1 (5b) in Cheddar Gorge, south-west England, "Cenotaph Corner" E1 (5b) on Dinas Cromlech in north Wales, "Tumbleweed Connection" E2 (5c) on Goat Crag in Borrowdale, The Lake District, "Yo Yo" E1 (5b) on the east face of Aonach Dubh in Glencoe, north-west Scotland.

BOULDERING GRADES

In Britain the purely technical numerical/adjectival grade is used, i.e. 5c, etc., and no separate system has as yet gained universal acceptance. However, the standard of bouldering varies tremendously from area to area and often there is little real comparison with a 5c boulder problem and a technical pitch to be found on a crag. Elsewhere in the world there are numerous systems of grading bouldering; in the USA a system B1 to B3 is used and in France four grades are assigned to the famous Courvier rocks at Fontainbleau near Paris which are designated by colours (painted on the rocks with the number of the individual problem) to represent an increasing order of difficulty – orange, blue, red and then white (some of the older "whites" are actually marked in black!). However, in each country that actually has a system grading the difficulty of boulder problems there are often further systems for individual areas (elsewhere in the Fontainbleau Forest the "colours" system of grading boulders is quite different!) And so all you can really do is discover the local system on arrival or study the guide beforehand.

In Britain there are many bouldering areas, particularly on gritstone. Brimham Rocks, Caley Crags and Almscliff all have famous boulder problems and in the Lake District the Bowderstone in Borrowdale provides bouldering on what is probably the single largest boulder in Britain.

WINTER GRADES

The British system is numerical, beginning with Grade 1 and proceeding in difficulty up to Grade VI. Local variations exist and this, in addition to the seasonal variance in conditions, means that all winter grades must be treated with caution. (Always leave a large safety margin when tackling a winter climb and climb well within your known ability and fitness.)

The following notes on the winter grades give an idea of what may be encountered:

GRADE I – These are straightforward gully climbs, easy angled buttresses, and average angled snow climbs. Cornice difficulties can be expected. (Often taken in descent by competent and experienced parties.)

GRADE II – Gullies with minor pitches, steep snow with difficult cornices and buttresses of greater difficulty than those under Grade 1.

GRADE III – Gullies containing at least one steep ice pitch and several minor ones. Sustained buttress climbs with possible short, technically hard sections.

GRADE IV – Generally steeper, more sustained climbs of a fairly serious nature. Long, steep ice pitches and/or difficult rock or mixed moves may be expected.

GRADE V – Serious climbs which may be sustained and technical; also highly technical but relatively well protected mixed routes.

GRADE VI – Routes which are harder still and which, all factors considered, make for an exceptionally difficult climb. This includes the climbing of technically difficult routes, with perhaps just a dusting of snow on them, using crampons and axe "hooking" and "torqueing" techniques.

ALPINE/FRENCH OVERALL GRADING

This overall rating system takes into consideration not only the technical difficulty and the seriousness of the individual pitches but also the overall seriousness of the route. This latter factor involves an assessment of the commitment required, the altitude, the total length of the route, the difficulty of the descent, etc.

The following ratings also have "superior" and "inferior" suffixes:

F – easy,
PD – slightly harder,
AD – fairly difficult,
D – harder,
TD – very hard,
ED – extremely hard,
ABO – abominable!

AID CLIMBING

A0 – involves the use of one or only a few points of aid and does not require the use of etriers.

A1 TO A5 – involves aid climbing where the sections may not be fixed and require all the specialist equipment and devices of the aid climber. It accounts for the length and commitment of a route, the nature of the rock and the fall potential if a point of aid "rips".

2
ROCK CLIMBING EQUIPMENT AND ITS USE

Climbing equipment design is a balance between light weight and strength (or function as is the case with clothing). Today, with modern materials available we have the benefit of extremely light equipment that is amply strong for the job it is intended to do. Here we will examine the main items of gear that are used by the rock and ice climber and discuss their use and limitations and how to care for them.

Remember that although climbing equipment is expensive it is nothing compared with the cost of a human life – it could be your life! So, get the right gear, treat it properly and discard it when it is worn out.

THE ROPES
Nylon rope should comply with the U.I.A.A. standard and if this is so it will be stated on the label. The only type of rope that is worth considering is kernmantel which consists of an inner core of multifibres enclosed in a woven sheath. There are many to choose from and there are a number of factors that will affect your choice in the shop.

The ropes and slings. Here there are three sewn standard length slings (0.45m, 0.6m and 1.2m in length) and the standard kernmental ropes: (A) 50m (10.5mm diameter); (B) 50m (9mm diameter); (C) 50m (8.5mm diameter). (Note the Alpine coiling.)

Having decided on diameter and length, don't just look at the price and colour but note the handling characteristics and the approximate number of leader falls a rope is fabricated to take. It should be noted that there can be no absolute indication here because each fall is different and any given figure is based on the premiss that there is no external damage to the rope caused by the rock or any other external influence. The number of U.I.A.A. falls will give you a relative standard; in turn this gives an indication about the number of recommended leader falls the rope is designed to take – after which it should be discarded – and hence it will give you some idea about how long you get for your money. (Basically each U.I.A.A. fall is based on a standard test: a drop of an 80 kg weight over 5 metres. It is actually a measurement of the severity of a fall, known as the "fall factor". This information is only a simple appraisal of a rather technical subject – to help the non-technically minded climber appreciate the limited life of a rope and the indication of this that can be gained from noting the U.I.A.A. fall number for any particular rope.)

Sensibly deciding just when a rope should be discarded is not easy: the rope may look visually OK (with no apparent signs of undue stretching, distortion or sheath damage) but it may be sufficiently weakened to the point where it may not be able to withstand a leader fall. There should be no element of doubt regarding the safety of a rope, of course, and the following information serves (along with regular observation and care) as a basic guide: for climbers using their ropes only occasionally, ropes can last 2-4 years; for those climbers who use their ropes most weekends and during holidays a rope could be expected to be used for about 2 years; for full-time rock climbers taking repeated falls on extreme climbs, professional climbers and guides a rope can be good for a much shorter period of something like 3 months to 1 year. Some ropes are treated chemically to "stay dry", although they are usually heavier, and this is a further consideration to bear in mind.

ROPE SIZE

Ropes are available in 45m(150ft) or 50m(165ft) lengths. The length of the rope obviously limits the length of the pitch. Pitches on traditional routes rarely exceed 45m but on harder, modern routes it is common to find 50m pitches; for the little extra weight and cost those few feet may save an embarrassing situation!

Diameter is another important consideration:

8. 5mm – can be used double in an Alpine situation where lightweight rope is essential. (I personally would not recommend this diameter rope to tackle high standard rock climbing.)

9mm – used double for any situation.

10. 5 mm to 11mm – can be used singly for all climbing warranting single rope technique.

ROPE CARE

(1) Be gentle to the rope on the rocks !Keep it protected from sharp edges and falling stones; the sheath cuts and abrades (wears) very quickly.
(2) Never run nylon against nylon (rope through sling or rope over rope in same crab) because it quickly loses strength and melts (or burns).
(3) Try to avoid running through acute angles when loaded, i.e. through a belay plate. (If this is done by necessity when abseiling, *go slowly*.)

(4) Never stand on a rope; to do so shows incompetence.

(5) Regularly inspect the sheath of a rope for any damage. This can occur in a number of different forms from a clean cut to an abrasion of the fibres. If the sheath is unduly damaged the rope must be discarded. Any damage that affects the core of a rope means the rope should be instantly discarded. Undue stretching of the rope weakens it and a rope thus affected should also be abandoned. (Note: during a fall the rope stretches and some time should be allowed after a severe fall to allow the rope to contract.)

(6) Keep the rope free from kinks.

(7) Avoid oily car boots! Keep away from chemicals and battery acid (this includes leakage from a damaged head torch battery).

(8) Store in a cool, dry and dark place (preferably hung freely) and keep away from heat, stoves, etc.

(9) If dirty, or to remove grit, ropes can be washed in luke warm water using a mild detergent.

(10) Only air dry the rope, away from strong sunlight and never use any artificial heat source.

(11) Remember that use, falls and time (exposure to sunlight) reduce the strength of the rope. When its time is up (very difficult to decide) use it only for towing the car.

(12) Mark the mid point of a rope with insulating tape as this serves as a very useful means of measuring pitch length etc.

SLINGS

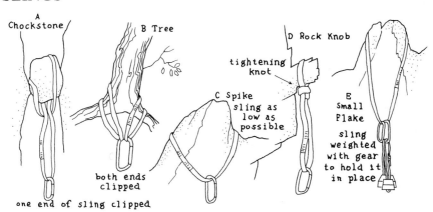

Slings used as anchors.

(A) This shows the sling threaded (around a chockstone jammed in a crack) and looped through itself, so tightening around the object it is threading. The crab is clipped to a single loop only. This can be beneficial, especially around a chockstone where the tape is situated in such a way to jam further between the choc and the edge of the crack. However, it is not as strong as the next method (B).

(B) Here the sling is simply wrapped around (threaded around a tree trunk or limb or through a natural feature) and both ends are clipped.

(C) Sling over spike or flake.

(D) Here the principle is the same as in (C), but the sling is knotted on tight to the object to keep it in place. It is often used on small rock spikes (nubins) and on granite "chicken heads".

(E) When small flakes are used as runner placements (small width flexible tape is placed over the top) in marginal situations (i.e. when there is nothing else!), it is usual to weight down slings with excess crabs and gear to keep them in place.

Firstly, it should be noted that many accidents have resulted from the knot in tape slings becoming undone and I would urge the climber to obtain the factory-sewn, stitched slings for these are the safest. In most cases they are better, too, for there is no bulky knot to contend with and so they are both lighter and stronger. Most slings used are tape slings, although line slings should be used for prusiking.

The standard lengths are 1. 2m, 0. 6m and 0. 45m and the thickness usually varies with the length. The width of tape should also be selected to match the particular type of crab that is to be used – too wide for any particular crab reduces the potential sling strength and overstresses the crab.

USES

They have many uses as anchors for both runners and main belays. Other important uses occur in prusiking and acting as an extension unit on runners.

CRABS

Crab is the most popular name now in use for what was more traditionally called the "karabiner". The terms "snaplink" or "biner" are other names used. Whatever the name, Crabs are an essential piece of equipment and come in many shapes and forms.

Crabs are a metal clip with a spring-loaded gate; they form a safe joining link between ropes and the other equipment needed on rock and ice climbs (clipping ropes to anchors or runners which may be slings [tapes or lines], nuts, pegs etc.) whilst allowing free passage of the rope through the link. The gate is easily opened inwards with light pressure from the climber's thumb (snapping shut on release) and once clipped the sling or rope (or both) remain there even in the event of a climber fall.

The various types, shapes and sizes you can expect when confronting crabs in a climbing shop are illustrated below.

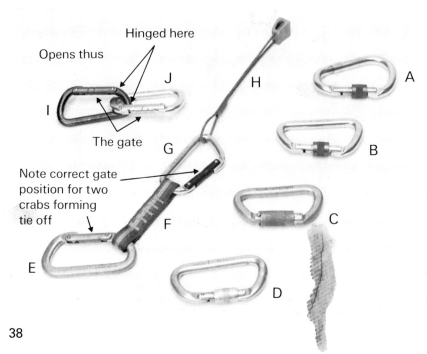

Hinged here
Opens thus
J
H
A
I
The gate
G
B
Note correct gate
position for two
crabs forming
tie off
F
C
E
D

Normally the light alloy Crabs are used for runners and the screwgate and locking Crabs (offering extra security) for belaying purposes.

SCREWGATE CRAB/LOCKING CRAB – used when extra security is required in a belay or main rope situation. The screwgate consists of a collar which fastens up, on a screw thread, to lock over the opening end of the gate. The locking crab releases the gate by rotation between finger and thumb; then, when released, it automatically locks. Mechanically, it is more complicated than the screwgate (there is more to go wrong) and involves a spring which can corrode, trap grit or freeze up, which, in turn, can cause it to jam. In addition to this, it is harder to operate with one hand and I personally prefer the simpler screwgate Crab.

PEAR-SHAPED SCREWGATE CRAB – used where the main climbing rope is to pass smoothly through the Crab, such as when belaying with a belay plate, or when using an Italian Hitch or when abseiling.

LIGHTWEIGHT ALLOY CRABS AND THE TIE-OFF – mainly used for runners and when the Crabs are clipped, as shown. To form a tie-off they should both be clipped in the relative direction illustrated here; that is, both are first clipped into the sling in the same way and then the bottom Crab is rotated around so that the gates are opposite. This is *absolutely essential* to give a quick opening of the gate and placement of the rope when on the lead.

CLIPPING TWO CRABS – sometimes this is done for speed if the tie-offs run out, but it is not good practice for there is a real *danger* that one of the main ropes can twist the crabs into a configuration where the rope opens a gate. (Note: this is also more likely in some Crabs which have, by design, curved gates to facilitate quick clipping.)

GATE CONSIDERATIONS – the gate is an integral part of the crab's design strength and it must be correctly closed (and kept closed) for the crab to function correctly. Always prevent any possibility of the gate being opened unintentionally after clipping with a Crab. This may involve rotating the Crab to move the gate away from projections. Ensure that any running rope does not run over the outside of a gate. Never clip a Crab so that load is being taken (for example, through a belay sling) directly by the gate – Crabs are designed to be loaded through their ends only. Failure to do this may easily result in the Crabs breaking under load.

GENERAL CLIPPING CONSIDERATIONS – without entering too deeply into theoretical design concepts it should be mentioned that the spine of a crab provides its main strength; the greater the leverage on this the more likely the possibility of crab failure. An important consideration, particularly when using lightweight crabs, is the fact that this leverage can be increased (and hence the possibility of crab failure) by clipping a tape sling/tie-off that is too wide or by clipping two ropes into one crab. Therefore avoid the possibility of overstressing lightweight crabs by only clipping slings of the right width and by only clipping a single rope.

(*Opposite*) Crabs and a tie-off.

(A) Pear-shaped alloy screwgate crab	(F) Tie-off sling (these come in various lengths)
(B) Alloy screwgate crab	(G) Lightweight alloy crab
(C) Alloy self-locking (twistlock) crab	(H) Nut runner on wire
(D) Hollow alloy screwgate crab	(I) Lightweight alloy crab
(E) Hollow alloy crab	(J) Light weight alloy crab

Combinations: (E) + (F) + (G) + (H) = complete runner, which consists of a nut (E) and two crabs clipped to a short sling (with two clipping eyes sewn either end) – the tie-off (F, G & H). (I) + (J) is known as a two-crab clip and is a poor alternative to the tie-off.

Never clip a hollow alloy Crab into either a wire sling or another Crab; they are designed to clip nylon only. Additionally, do not use the hollow alloy screwgate in an abrasive situation, i.e. with a belay plate or when abseiling.

A further point to note when considering which Crab to purchase is the width of the upper lip (where the top of the gate sits); when the gate is open and the Crab is being clipped into bolts or pegs will this lip be small enough to fit easily through the hanger or eye? (Some are very thick, for strength, but will not clip gear because they are too wide.)

CRAB CARE

Crabs are pretty resilient, if used correctly, and even if dropped they are safe if there is no visible damage (cracks or distortion). This is true for the solid type only. Hollow Crabs are much more susceptible to buckling forces if only slightly dinted and if suspect they must be discarded.

The alloy in Crabs is based on aluminium and is prone to salt attack; always clean (wash in clean, non-salt water) and then spray with a suitable lubricant (such as WD 40)after use in a sea cliff environment. In any case crabs should be regularly inspected, for abrasion as well as failure (cracks or distortion), and lubricated to give smooth gate action. It is better to lubricate with a chemical spray rather than liquid oil, for the latter inevitably finds its way onto the nylon ropes and slings – a situation to be avoided.

Identification/personalisation is best done with distinctive insulation tape. Gates (solid Crabs only) can be lightly marked with a file or stamped with a punch to give the owner's mark. Although this obviously weakens the gate by some finite amount it is acceptable if done sensibly and in moderation. In no circumstances should it be done to the body of the Crab through which the main stress (in the event of loading) is distributed.

HARNESSES

Today, particularly in high standard rock climbing where it is normal both to fall off and belay leader and second falls, a climbing harness is an important item of equipment. It is as fundamental as the Crabs and ropes.

The most useful harness system consists of a waist belt and leg loops. These can be permanently joined (as is the case with the harness shown on the left of the diagram) or there may be a temporary linking system enabling the leg loop/waist belt combination to be changed around or the waist belt to be worn alone (shown by harness on the right). The permanent system is usually the simplest to put on and for this reason alone I prefer it. There are other harness sytems, the chest harness and full body harness for example, but for the normal climbing situation the waist belt/ leg loop harness system is the best.

USES

The harness transmits and distributes the climber's load, both static and dynamic in the case of a fall. For the falling climber it means all the weight and shock of the fall is distributed around his/her body, legs and waist. Traditionally, this was done by the rope being tied around the waist and it was an extremely painful and dangerous business, but today's harnesses enable the climber to fall, and be held on the rope, in absolute comfort. This depends, of course, on one's particular anatomical

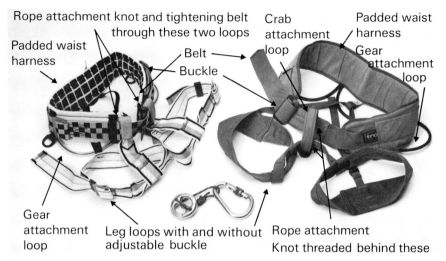

Rope attachment knot and tightening belt through these two loops

Padded waist harness

Belt

Buckle

Crab attachment loop

Padded waist harness

Gear attachment loop

Gear attachment loop

Leg loops with and without adjustable buckle

Rope attachment Knot threaded behind these

Two climbing harnesses, with padded waist belts and leg loops, and belay plate and crab.

peculiarities! A climber can hang from a rope in a correctly fitting harness for many hours (days if necessary), with the main weight distribution being taken around the thighs and bottom – you can dangle from the nose of El Capitan (in Yosemite, California where multi-day ascents are the norm) with all the comfort of sitting in the armchair (well, perhaps rocking chair) at home.

A belayer holding a fall simply has the load transmitted through the belay plate and crab (illustrated between the harnesses in the diagram above) and then through the harness, partly to the climber's body (the belayer's dead weight partly counters leader fall) and partly to the anchor. A modern harness, with waist and leg loops, then permits the considerable stresses and loading experienced in climbing to be taken in both comfort and safety.

CHOICE

There are many types of harness on the market and it is up to the individual to choose the harness that meets his/her personal requirements. The two harnesses illustrated (there are many others) are suitable for rock climbing but in ice climbing, where the climber must don the harness over crampons, etc., it may be desirable to choose a harness with more easily adjustable, or opening, leg loops so the cramponed boot does not have to be placed through the loop. This feat can be quite tricky even in ideal conditions, let alone balancing one-legged on sloping ice with a blizzard swirling around your head. Some ice climbers prefer to use the waist belt only, abandoning the leg loops, sacrificing the degree of comfort and safety in the event of a fall for the sake of speed and simplicity.

Weight versus padding (around the waist only) is one consideration and another is the positioning of the gear loops for clipping on all those runners the brave leader is going to carry. Ensure they are placed so you can both clip on a reasonable quantity of gear (enough carrying capacity) and unclip it on the climb without trouble (correctly positioned). You will be paying enough money for the harness so make sure it's suitable before leaving the shop; you shouldn't have to start modifying it later.

41

FIT

Get a harness that fits you not only in the shop but after you have donned all that clothing you are going to wear when the sun disappears. Harnesses are adjustable but only within their particular size range; there are usually three sizes: small, medium and gorilla. If a particular harness fits you, and others do not seem to, then, despite other considerations, that harness may well be the most suitable choice.

IMPORTANT CONSIDERATIONS

Make sure you know about the particular harness you purchase by carefully reading the instructions and, preferably, by asking the shop assistant to demonstrate all the features:

THE BUCKLE FASTENING – requires the belt first to be threaded through the complete buckle and then taken back through the first slot. (The entire safety of the harness depends on this.)

ATTACHING THE ROPE(S) – again each harness has its own system but check out carefully that you are doing it right for that particular harness. I prefer the system, being an absolute coward and an old one at that, where even if the buckle should fail the rope still holds the harness together and in place. This is the case with the harness on the left in the photograph on page 41 where the ropes are threaded horizontally through two loops (attached to the waist belt and leg loops), as does the fastening belt. With the harness on the right the rope is threaded vertically around both the waist belt and the leg loop.

Also, when tying on, do it directly with rope to harness without an intermediate Crab. This is based on the very sound, general principle that the least complicated and the simpler the system, the less there is to go wrong and the safer it is. (You may have noticed by now that all my rules are based on cowardice – they work well!)

ATTACHING THE BELAY PLATE CRAB, ABSEIL CRAB OR ANCHOR CRAB – this should always be a screwgate or locking type Crab. Again, I try to keep the system as safe as possible and clip the loop formed by the rope attachment knot. With the harness illustrated on the right, this is not so easy because this knot is running vertically and it can be seen that there is a stitched loop designed for the purpose. However, remember the point about simplicity and failure. Abseiling and the like (prusiking, etc.) means that the load must be attached to the harness via a Crab, because the climber in most cases will not be tied onto the ropes.

ROPE MANAGEMENT HARDWARE

These are the mechanical systems used in controlling a loaded rope as in belaying, abseiling and descending.

ROCK CLIMBING HARDWARE

The basic kit for the free rock climber consists of equipment for making the climb safe. It comprises the various components that make up a runner (slings, nuts, tie-offs and Crabs), the belay plate with screwgate Crab, chalk bag (for carrying climber's chalk) and an extractor(s) for removing any jammed nuts. Remember, a climber can rely on his nut protection to prevent injury if a fall occurs, providing his nuts stay in place.

THE NUT RUNNER

It is useful, to help understand the mechanics of nut runner placements, to know something of the origin of "the nut". In Britain the original concept of a runner (a "running belay") came with the threading of naturally *in situ* chockstones when they appeared on a pitch. It was as late as the 1950s before climbers realised that carrying a selection of pebbles in the pocket enabled, by jamming them in the cracks and then threading a sling, runners to be placed, more or less, where they were needed. This graduated to threading actual nuts, with their screw threads drilled out, onto slings and carrying these until the climber could insert them in a suitable crack. That was a big step and when survival expert Tony Greenbank took his nut assortment to America and climbed Bastile Crack with Royal Robbins the idea was rapidly passed on to Yvon Chouinard who grasped the potential and developed the concept – the

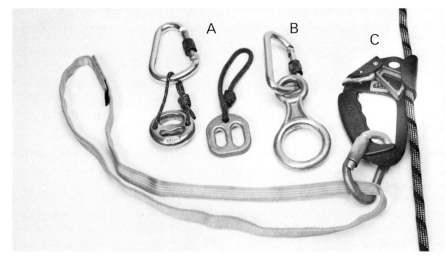

Rope management hardware
(A) shows two belay plates (on the left is the 'Bettabrake' and on the right is the original belay plate – the Sticht Plate). The one on the left is clipped via a 5mm line to a pear-shaped screwgate crab. Note that the length of line (approx. 1ft (300mm) total length) is an integral part of the system, is not just a carrying loop and is essential for safe belaying. When the rope is clipped into the system (see "Rope techniques") it is this line that prevents the plate from riding up the main rope out of reach (it does not take any load, however). The Sticht Plate can have slots to take either a 9mm rope or an 11mm rope or, most usefully, one 11mm and one 9mm rope (this plate is shown here), which in practice serves to take two 9mm ropes or a single 11mm rope. The Bettabrake is dual purpose and will take either diameter ropes. Of all the plates I have tried I find that the Sticht allows the easiest running of the ropes when the belayer is taking in or letting out the ropes. The Sticht is available with a spring which facilitates easy feeding through of the ropes and is a most useful addition.
(B) shows the figure of eight descender, probably the safest and best of all abseil devices, clipped to a screwgate crab. Note that it is best to use the figure of eight as shown in "Rope techniques", but if it is necessary to abseil on a single 9mm the rope can be placed in the small loop and the crab clipped in the larger one. This gives more mechanical friction and slows down the descent.
(C) shows a mechanical ascender for "jugging" up the rope. Placed thus, it will slide up the rope in only one direction. The trigger mechanism (needs two operations to remove from the rope), when released, enables the ascender to move freely in either direction on the rope. Note how the crab and sling are clipped at the bottom of the handle – the furthest distance from the point of contact on the rope. The hole at the top is used for carrying or when using the ascender for purposes other than jugging up the rope.

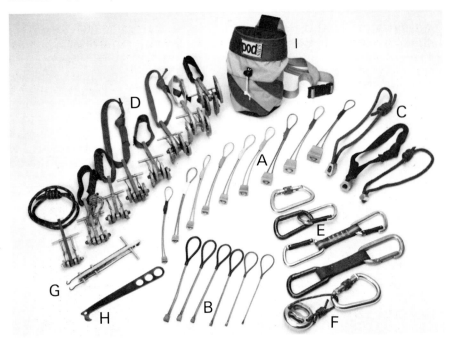

A critical selection of equipment which the free rock climber requires to protect a climb with nut runners.

(A) Rocks, sizes 1 to 9 on wire
  and (on right) size 7 on rope
(B) RPs, sizes 0 to 5
(C) Hexcentrics on tape and rope
(D) Friends, sizes 1/2 to 4

(E) Crabs and tie-offs
(F) Belay plate and pear-shaped screwgate crab
(G) BB friend extractor
(H) Nut key
(I) Chalk bag and carrying belt

modern nut was born. Today nuts are made from light alloy and incorporate a number of ingenious design features to provide the rock climber with a variable protection system that is highly transportable and one which can be inserted and removed without damaging the rock.

There is a wide variety of available hardware. The following basic nuts fill most requirements for most of the time.

ROCKS

The diagram below illustrates a set of Rocks from size 1 to 9 on wire and a size 7 on rope (it is usual to have sizes 7 upwards on rope because of their flexibility). Rocks are the most popular and widely useful nut. Their design is based on the old wedge principle but they are somewhat

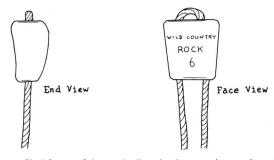

The profiled faces of the rock allow both camming and wedging.

ingeniously refined to incorporate a rocking (camming) action, through their curved faces, which really does lock them into the cracks. If you imagine the nut rocking on the convex (outwardly curved) face and "gripping" the crack with the other concave face, then you will have some understanding of the mechanics that make rocks work – this in turn will help you select sound placements.

Placing Rocks

In vertical cracks the curved faces can be placed to the rock (real rock!), end on placement as viewed, and this is the best placement, giving both wedging and camming action. Alternatively the ends can be placed to the rock, face on as viewed, which gives wedging action only.

End on – both camming and wedging

Face on – wedging action only

Rock placement in vertical cracks. End on gives wedging and camming security; face on gives only wedging security.

Placing in horizontal or diagonal cracks should generally only be done one way – that is with the outwardly curved (convex) face down, for this will provide camming action when the nut is loaded.

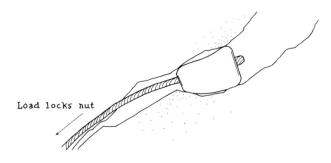

Load locks nut

Placing a rock in a horizontal or diagonal crack.
The general rule is: outwardly curved face down.

Removal
Taking Rocks out can be problematical and they are probably the most difficult of nuts to remove, particularly if they have been loaded or fallen on. The following general remarks can be applied to the removal of all nuts.

Don't yank wildly at the sling or wire; this only locks the nut tighter. Loosen the nut with the fingers; if this is not possible, free it by tapping with a Crab or tapping or levering with the nut key (see photograph on page 44). It is usual for the second man always to carry a nut key. Once the nut moves it can be guided out using the wire (or tape). Always follow the path of placement, shouting up to the leader for guidance if necessary.

Another good technique when all else fails is to clip a long sling to the nut wire (or sling) and to whip it up and down – this is surprisingly effective.

Care
Visual inspection and washing in fresh water after use near the sea is all that is required. Watch for broken strands of wire and when this occurs throw them away! These comments apply to all nuts.

RPS
An RP is a small wedging nut which goes down to very small sizes. The nut is of relatively soft metal (brass) and this distorts, and therefore grips, the rock rugosities when the nut is loaded. It is a very useful nut for extreme climbing but the size obviously limits its strength.

Placing RPs
The nuts provide wedging and distortion grip properties only. Otherwise, placement considerations are as for those of the Rock.

HEXCENTRICS
Two Hexcentrics are illustrated (p. 44) on flexible tape and line. These are really a progression from the original drilled out nuts but the design has now moved on to include camming action properties (they are good for placing in pockets and irregular fissures in the rock) and these properties are best exploited when the nut is threaded with flexible tape or line.

Typical hexcentric placement in a pocket.

FRIENDS

D (p. 44) illustrates a set of Friends from size ½ up to 4, in half sizes. They are an expanding cam device where four spring-loaded cams, contracted using the trigger bar (two fingers either side of the shaft and thumb on the base of the shaft), are released to grip either side of a crack or pocket (two sets of cams acting in opposition). It is probably wisest to buy them with machine-sewn slings already *in situ* and the Crab is then clipped directly to this and the rope to form the complete runner. This protection device revolutionised the runner game and made fearfully dangerous cracks, even those through horizontal roofs, into havens of security. Designed by American Ray Jardine, they received their ultimate accolade in a letter to *Mountain* magazine in which a climber thanked Ray for saving his life: climbing a granite crack the area was subject to an earthquake; despite the whole cliff shaking and the crack widening, resulting, naturally enough, in the climber falling, the Friends held fast and simply expanded with the crack!

Placing Friends

So long as all four of the expanding cams press rock (in a crack or pocket) before they reach their point of full extension the Friend will hold fast. In practice try to get all four cams equally expanded, as this is the most stable placement, and "test" the placement with a gentle but firm tug on the sling/Crab. Whenever possible Friends should be positioned to resist best the directional forces of any impending fall.

The most secure placement is in a horizontal crack but in this position the leverage on the stem should be reduced as much as possible.

Friends work even when placed upside down in a tapered crack – although this is the worst case placement, of course.

47

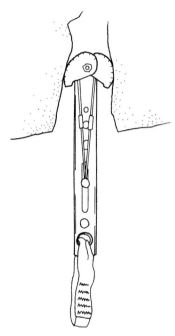

A perfect Friend placement in a regular vertical crack. All four cams are expanded equally.

The Friend, the ultimate protection device, placed in an upside-down tapering crack. This is not recommended if there is an alternative placement!

Friend placed in a horizontal crack. Here a rope thread has been tied through one of the holes in the stem and the crab has been clipped to reduce the leverage.

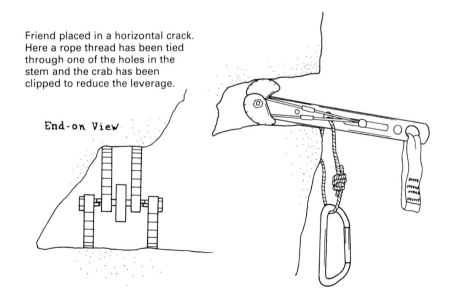

End-on View

Cam positioning. Due consideration should be given to the positioning of the inner and outer cams to maximise the seating area.

A further point for consideration in placing a friend, perhaps for simplicity in a vertical crack, is the fact that there are inner cams on one side of the shaft and outer cams on the other. Therefore, if the rock on either side of the crack is at a different "level", i.e. one side is further away than the other, then the inner cams should be placed on the side which presents the smallest face as per the diagram at the foot of p. 48.

Careful thought when placing a Friend should also be given to its subsequent removal; one of the vices of a Friend is that, under certain circumstances, it will walk into a crack, due to pressure from the rope or inadvertent action by a climber. This can make it extremely difficult to remove because it becomes increasingly hard for the aspirant remover to get his fingers around the trigger as the device recedes into the depths of a narrow crack.

A further problem to be avoided when placing is that of bottoming. If a Friend is placed hard against the bottom of a crack it can be almost impossible to remove it. This is because the removal action requires the shaft to be moved fractionally relative to the cams (and hence the Friend to be moved back into the crack) before the trigger can be depressed, the cams contracted and the Friend withdrawn.

Removal

As stated above, to remove the Friend the trigger is depressed and the Friend is withdrawn. If the Friend has received shock loading, i.e. has held a fall, it may require a sharp blow on the base of the shaft at the same time as the trigger is depressed. This is achieved (presumably the remover has only one pair of hands) by hooking two loops of wire (two wire nut runners) over each end of the trigger shaft and pulling.

If the Friend has *walked* into the crack, as described above, and the trigger bar is within the crack then this same wire trick is applicable. It is much better, however, to use the BB Friend Extractor. It is a simple but extremely effective device.

Never attempt to remove a Friend by smashing at it with a hammer. This is a thoroughly stupid action which only results in the Friend being destroyed. Leave it to someone more skilled in the art of removal or better equipped with an extractor.

Care

Aluminium alloy should be washed and lubricated after use near the sea. Lubricate the cam springs regularly with a suitable spray (WD 40). The cam pull wires often wear through and to mend this and other damage the manufacturer (Wild Country) offers a refurbishment service.

CHALK

Chalk is light magnesium carbonate and is popular in the block form.

I well remember the headline "Allen Climbs Great Wall Free – But Uses Chalk!" At the time I thought, "Good effort – so what?" And so it has proved to be; most high standard rock climbers now use chalk on hard routes. It improves the grip and works when the hands are sweaty or if the rock is damp or even if the hands are cold (another case of strange but true). As a guideline, in Britain it is not considered reasonable to use chalk on routes that are less than Hard Very Severe in standard. Although it whitens the rock, in most cases it washes away with the first rain.

Resin is an alternative to chalk and this is popular in some bouldering areas where it is thought bad practice to mark the whereabouts of holds with white chalk marks.

CARRYING

A well-designed chalk bag is illustrated in the photograph on page 57; because of the flexible mid section the chalk stays put in the bag when placed on the belt around the climber's waist (allowing it to be slid to where the climber wishes to dip). Even when the climber leaves the vertical, the neck stays open and is wide enough to allow easy access with the hand. It fastens with a draw cord at the mid-point, so allowing easy opening, and it is pile lined to distribute the chalk on the climber's sweaty fingers.

GEAR COMBINATIONS AND LOAD SHARING

In a number of circumstances it is necessary to arrange a combination of nuts to form a stable runner and in other cases two nuts, which individually would not take the required loading, have to share the load equally to work.

Gear combination. Two runners are used in opposition: placed in a horizontal crack, as illustrated, they will stay *in situ* to resist a fall; placed singly, they would not stay put. A better linkage system here, i.e. to reduce the diversification of load to the various components, would be to clip crab to crab.

(p. 51, top left)
Load sharing. If used for a rock anchor when belaying, it is always better to have two separate slings of equal length, i.e. two separate units so that if one fails the other will instantly take the load.
Note very carefully that the single sling clipped thus results automatically in equal distribution of the load. However, it is *crucial* to slip the sling in such a fashion that it remains clipped to the body of the sling should one anchor fail. This is achieved by first forming the sling into a figure of eight (simply by crossing one end over) and then clipping the crab through the cross point into both loops. It is clipped as shown in the next photograph.

(p. 51, top right)
Correct clipping of a single load sharing sling. It is simple to achieve by crossing the end of the sling over to form a figure of eight. The two loops are clipped to the anchors and the rope crab is clipped through the crossover point.

PEGS

Rock pegs (pitons) come in many shapes and sizes in both hard and soft steel. Hard steel pegs can be re-used many times, which explains their importance in aid climbing big walls. Soft steel pegs are considerably cheaper, although they have a limited life. Hard steel pegs penetrate razor thin cracks but soft steel ones have the capacity to deform to the crack shape and hence they have good holding power. Generally hard rock requires hard steel pegs and soft rock, soft steel pegs.

Hard steel pegs begin to develop longitudinal cracks before failure; soft steel pegs can snap without warning.

Use of pegs should be kept to an absolute minimum. Always use a nut in preference, because pegs do considerable damage to the rock and, left in place, they eventually rust away.

PLACING

Pegs are designed to be hammered in cracks in the rock and were once referred to as "nails". They were immortalised in Paul Ross's song, "All For Want Of A Nail". They are most secure when placed in horizontal cracks but each different type of peg is designed to be used in a specific way and the diagram below, with the accompanying notes, should be studied.

Pegs are placed by hammering, and experience is necessary to know when to stop because overdriving produces a negative effect on their stability (strength and holding power). As pegs begin to hold to their maximum power they produce an increasingly high pitched ringing. When this distinctive ring is heard it is time to stop hammering or overdriving will result.

REMOVAL

Hammer the peg first to one side (up or down the crack) and then to the other, taking the peg as far as it will go each time. Then give it a few extra hard blows, until it can be pulled out with the fingers.

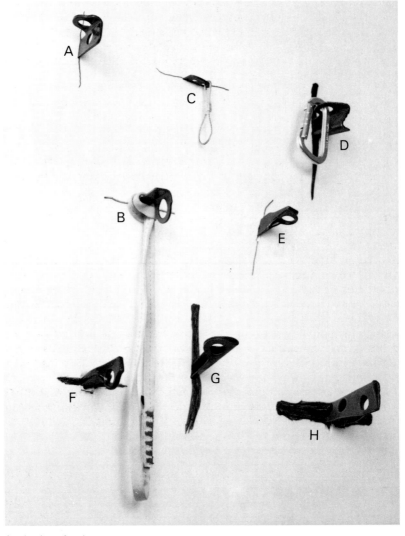

A selection of rock pegs.

(A) Knife blade	(D) Leeper	(G) Channel
(B) Knife blade	(E) Blade	(H) Large channel (bong)
(C) RURP	(F) Angle Blade	

In the photograph above, (A) illustrates a hard steel knife blade placed in a vertical crack.

(B) illustrates a knife blade placed in a horizontal crack (placing a peg in a horizontal crack is more secure than a vertical placement). This peg has been tied off with a sling using a lark's foot knot to reduce the leverage.

(C) illustrates a RURP (Realised Ultimate Reality Piton) placed horizontally in a wafer-thin crack. This peg is suitable to take static load only and was developed for high standard aid climbing. It is made from hard steel and requires nerves of a similar nature to use it!

(D) illustrates a leeper placed in a vertical crack. This corrugated hard steel peg is extremely versatile and is suitable for the shallow cracks in

British mountain crags. Note carefully the position of the eye, clipped with crab, placed above the body of the peg. Loading of this peg through the eye twists it into the rock and hence increases the holding power.

(E) and (F) illustrate a blade in a vertical and horizontal crack respectively. It is another versatile peg and is produced in a number of sizes and lengths and in both hard and soft steel.

(G) illustrates a channel in a vertical crack. It was originated by Warren Harding from the legs of a pot-bellied stove and accounts for the famous section on The Nose of El Capitan (in Yosemite) called The Stove Leg Cracks.

(H) illustrates a bong placed correctly in a horizontal crack. This peg is just a large channel. When channels are placed horizontally they should stand with their open face (split side of the stove leg) to the bottom.

BOLTS

There are a number of different proprietary bolting systems. Climbing and caving shops sell the complete kits required (with a full set of instructions). Probably the best system is an expansion bolt whereby a hole is drilled into the rock, using a self drilling bolt which is held in one hand with a suitable holder and hammered with the other. Another system uses a percussion drill where rotation of the drill bit and blowing, to clean out rock dust, should be done at regular intervals. After this the body (sleeve) of the bolt, with a steel cone placed in the hole first, is driven in. The hard cone expands the soft aluminium sleeve and jams it into the hole. The sleeve is threaded and a bolt with a suitable hanger (eye to which the Crab is clipped) is screwed into place (a spanner is used to tighten it).

If you must place a bolt (see later for ethical considerations), then make it a good one. Place it in clean, strong rock and drill the hole deep enough. Remember that what you are doing is permanent and to this end use stainless steel components that will not rust away.

FRICTION BOOTS

Choosing the right climbing boot is one of the most important decisions the free rock climber will make when purchasing gear. Friction boots for free climbing, with their "super sticky" rubber, are so good and so specialised that there has almost come a point (when climbing the hardest grades) at which boots with different properties can be selected for different rock types — if you can afford it, that is!

PERFORMANCE

Let's face it, a rock climber wants achievement and in my experience whatever qualities a boot may lack if it is a top performer then that is the boot most climbers will go for. So, what do you look for in performance?

The answer is a boot that will perform better than any other all (or some depending on the nature of the climb to be tackled) of those footwork techniques discussed in "Climbing techniques". In practice, boots tend to have two main qualities: stiffness, which gives edging and straight-on toe holding ability, and smearing, which gives maximum grip. To some degree these qualities do not complement each other in boot construction. Therefore, it is necessary (if the climber uses only one pair of friction boots) to purchase boots that offer performance compatible with the climber's style or aspirations. It is pointless buying a superb edging boot to climb friction slabs or a good smearing boot to climb pocketed overhanging walls. However, as most climbers will climb both and have only one pair of boots to achieve the best overall performance they must sacrifice absolute performance in one or other fields (edging or smearing). Before the climb is commenced it is usual for the rock climber to spit on and rub the soles of the boots to make them warm and tacky – so increasing the sticking qualities of the boots. When they begin to squeak you are ready to go.

Free rock climbing boots. The boots on the left offer longitudinal and lateral stiffness, which makes them good for edging, and toe pockets. The boots on the right, the "Fire" boots, are possibly the best known smearing boots and are certainly some of the best boots for all-round performance. Both types of boot, as do other similar sorts, offer good overall performance. Friction demands that boots are clear and dry; the cleaning towel shown is an essential piece of equipment.

OTHER CONSIDERATIONS

Fit and comfort are very important. Again, they do not necessarily complement each other. It all depends on the type of climbing you intend to undertake. If you are going to tackle long multi-pitch routes comfort is the most important consideration. Short, hard, technical test pieces demand absolute performance and comfort may be secondary here. But you may pay the price, for many old climbers, such as myself, have perfect examples of "PA feet", a deformity induced by cramming feet into a certain kind of rock boot.

To confuse the issue further, it is important to remember that once you leave the shop, even if it fits when new, a boot may not fit after it has been worn a few times! Some boots stretch with use and become so slack as to be useless for high standard climbing, whereas some boots shrink, making them unbearably tight. The best advice is to talk to other climbers before making a purchase and to go to a shop where staff will tell you honestly (by having real practical knowledge about the product) about the properties of the boots they are selling.

Quality of manufacture and materials is also another consideration; boots are expensive and should last at least one season!

CARE

Boots can generally be resoled and re-randed. Friction boots should be kept as dry as possible and if sodden with rain should be air dried but not next to too strong a heat source (such as a fire or stove). Stuffing with newspaper to soak up the water is a useful tip. Keep the soles clean (wash the soles only) by using an absorbent towel as illustrated. Another point to watch is the effects of salt water on the eyelets: they can begin to corrode. If dipped in the sea, then selective washing of the eyelets in clean water is a good idea.

CRAG APPROACH GEAR

This depends, of course, on the location but I will split this category into three groups which constitute the main items of required gear: sacs, footwear and clothing.

SACS (RUCKSACKS)

Size, ancillary equipment (gear loops), etc. depend on just where you are going and with how much. When you make your decision you should bear in mind the conditions to which you are going to subject the sac. Remember, however, that one sac will probably be expected to fill a multitude of roles, from summer rock climbing through to Alpinism, but the problem with having a sac of ample volume is that you always seem to manage to fill it; it is a wise man who carries a limited capacity sac for it is he who travels light.

Crag approach gear. Illustrated are two medium-sized sacs of good repute and two types of popular approach footwear.

Sac Comfort and Durability

It is not only important that the sac takes all you wish it to carry but that it does so in comfort. There are some excellent sacs on the market and it is a good guide to rely on the manufacturer's name and reputation. A great deal of quality workmanship and materials make up a dependable sac. Although the style and colour may look appealing, there are a number of short cuts that can be taken, so producing an inferior and less durable product. The choice is yours but be warned. A sac should last a lifetime; some do, some don't.

Comfort is achieved through design (padding and style) and good personal fit (correct sizing and adjustment for load). Look for sacs offering easily adjustable straps, compression straps and waist belt. Examine the quality of construction at the most critical points: is the shoulder strap/sac join going to take repeated heavy loading; is the base of the sac going to take the abrasion and pounding it will receive when repeatedly dumped on the ground, fully loaded with gear, at the foot of the crag?

Care

Most good sacs require little maintenance and the best manufacturers offer a refurbishment and repair service. This is an important point to check when purchasing.

Carrying and Packing

The comfort and ease of carrying are directly affected by the manner in which you pack the sac. Try to keep everything inside, despite the external gear loops, as this keeps the sac balanced. It is an important point when you consider the rough terrain you are likely to cross. Pack the sac tightly, placing the heaviest items at the bottom, and keep the uncomfortably shaped items (hammers and boots, for example) away from the back section. Take up the slack in the sac with the compression straps, so stabilising the load. Finally, and irreverently, a good kick up the back works wonders!

FOOTWEAR

Suitable wear for rough terrain varies from the trainer, illustrated left, to the lightweight boot, illustrated right. If one accepts that the feet are most probably going to get wet on a mountain approach, then the trainer is a good and comfortable item of approach footwear. There are of course trainers and trainers and basically you get what you pay for. Avoid slippery soles (cleated good quality rubber, as illustrated, is most suitable for mountain terrain) and too much absorbing cushion under the heel. Some trainers designed for road running are unsuitable and it is easy to turn an ankle in rough terrain if wearing this type of shoe.

Lightweight boots are more traditional wear for the mountains and have the benefit of ankle support and water resistance. In fact, most lightweight boots are suitable for free rock climbing up to, say, Severe standard and their use is a worthwhile consideration for someone wishing to save weight on a mountain approach. (I climbed my first two HVSs in bendy walking boots, but I can't say I recommend it!)

Care

Air dry away from direct heat sources (such as fire or stove) and, if sodden, packing with newspaper overnight is a good tip. Clean by washing or brushing. Leather boots require additional care; the leather needs to be fed (lubricated) and waterproofed (unless the boot is the type impregnated with a silica cocktail) and all this can be achieved with a number of proprietary compounds such as G-WAX.

CLOTHING

It can be cold in the hills and on the crags. Have an adequate number of warm clothes and waterproofs for the season, even if they are kept in reserve in the sac. I tend to approach, at a rapid pace, clad in as little as possible, which often means just shorts and T shirt. On arrival at the crag these are usually wringing wet with perspiration and I discard them for clean and dry gear in the sac. Both items are light and crumple into virtually nothing, so having spare is no problem (true also for socks).

LEAD CLIMBER READY TO GO

Julia is an extreme rock climber about to start on a full 50-metre pitch of some variety and difficulty. It may seem that a certain amount of strength is required in those arms to carry all this gear and to climb the pitch. Indeed, it is, but the rack is typical for a difficult British crag climb.

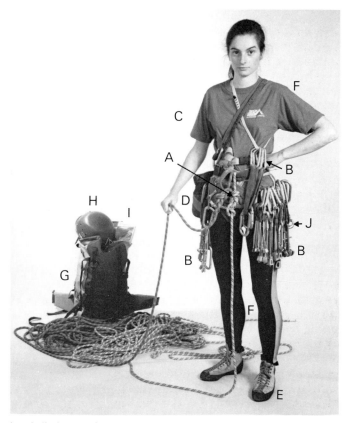

Lead climber ready to go.

(A) Double ropes to harness	(D) Chalk bag	(G) Sac
(B) The gear	(E) Friction boots	(H) Helmet
(C) Long sling	(F) Clothing	(I) Guidebook

Let's examine all the individual components previously discussed, showing how they are fitted together and carried in the practical situation.

(A) illustrates double ropes (two 50m, 9mm ropes) threaded and tied to the harness with figure of eight knots. (Note the Stopper Knot.)

(B) illustrates how the gear, nut runners and tie-offs, are racked up. Some tie-offs are placed to the left and some to the right, and some are placed around the neck on a bandolier. Nuts are carried in ascending size, again to left and right, with the smallest at the front. Friends are placed behind the nuts with different sizes on each side. Experience and the actual gear that is required on a pitch dictate just how it is racked and, of course, every one has his/her own particular system. The main thing is to know by routine just where everything is situated and to be able to remove it quickly and efficiently.

It is usual to have a range of nuts on one Crab, e.g. Rocks 1 to 3, and when the nut is placed to return the Crab with the remaining nuts to the harness. The placed nut is then clipped with a tie-off and, in turn, the rope is clipped into this. The runner is complete. Alternatively, a slightly quicker variation, if the second is alert and lets the slack rope through quickly enough, is to clip the tie off into the rope and then clip the placed nut.

57

Here tie-offs are clipped into a short sling around the neck and this is acting as a *bandolier*. (Note the first tie-off on the bandolier has the Crabs clipped correctly, but the bottom Crab still requires rotating to obtain the tie-off arrangement that gives optimum clipping ability, i.e. so the gates are arranged best to clip both nut and rope: see the photograph on page 38 for detail.) Some climbers like to have the gear situated clipped from a sling around the neck, but I prefer it situated down on the gear loops of the harness. Whatever your choice, clip the gear on in the direction shown, i. e. with the gate of the Crab to the body, because this facilitates the easiest removal. All these details enhance the speed and efficiency with which the leader places and clips his/her protection, which in turn makes an ascent safer and neater.

(C) illustrates a long sling carried and clipped correctly for easy one-handed removal that does not require lifting over the head and so avoids possible entanglement with other gear/slings around the neck. It is fastened by just clipping both ends of the loop. To remove, unclip, one-handed, one loop, and the sling will pull through ready for use.

(D) illustrates the chalk bag which should easily slide around the body for use by either hand.

(E) illustrates friction boots. Clean them before starting off. Many climbers give them a vigorous rubbing with spit and the hand until they squeak; at this point they have reached optimum cleanliness and temperature for top performance (this is like performing a warm-up lap in Formula 1 car racing!)

(F) illustrates light and flexible clothing suitable for climbing rock smoothly. Julia is wearing a rather splendid pair of lycra stretch tights and a neatly cut light cotton T–shirt which is colourful and stylish. The rest of the gear is in the sac ready to be donned.

On British crags it really is necessary, even in the height of summer, to have some warm clothing and waterproofs ready to hand. Climbing performance relies on the climber (and his/her muscles) being suitably warm: the point is that the rock climber must remain highly mobile and the warm clothing must be light and flexible. I prefer nylon track suit bottoms and always keep a fibre pile jacket and woolly hat to hand for those odd times the sun disappears.

(G) illustrates the sac. For rock climbing in Britain this usually remains at the foot of a climb.

(H) illustrates a climbing helmet. Although the wearing of a helmet is not popular in rock climbing, particularly in high standard rock climbing, there is absolutely no doubt that its use provides some protection. Statistics show that many tragedies, resulting from stonefall and climber fall, could have been avoided if a helmet had been worn. The choice is yours.

(I) illustrates the guidebook. If the route can be memorised it is better to leave the book behind, because it is awkward to carry. Some climbers drill a hole through the top near the spine of the book and thread a sling through, enabling the book to be clipped to the harness like any other piece of gear.

(J) illustrates the belay plate clipped to the back of the harness out of the climber's way – don't forget it. (The second should carry a nut key in addition to this.)

3

ICE CLIMBING
EQUIPMENT AND ITS USE

Much of what has been covered in "Rock climbing equipment and its use", the ropes, runners, etc., applies to climbing in winter and the ice climber must assimilate this information in addition to that given here. Use of axes and crampons and the full range of techniques used in climbing snow and ice are explained later, but here I will detail the individual items of equipment.

By necessity climbing ice or snow is a more mechanical game than pure rock climbing and the climber should carefully familiarise himself with the following items of equipment before attempting to use them in earnest. Test their weight and feel, swing the axes and attach the crampons to the boots, but don't cut off your ear or stab yourself in the leg!

AXES

In the past, as the going got steeper, the traditional long axe got shorter and the angle of inclination of the pick dropped from the horizontal to hook, puncture and grip the ice more effectively. Now on steep technical routes it is correct procedure to carry the short specialist axes (alternatively referred to as "tools", which usually means both the "axe" and the "hammer"). Unfortunately, for moving on moderately steep ground (see "Techniques") they have severe limitations, to some extent compensated by superior crampon-work. However, on mixed terrain of only moderate steepness (this expression is defined in the techniques section and includes snow up to 50 degrees inclination – which in fact is pretty steep when you look down!) where fast, safe movement is desirable the single, longer (more traditional) ice axe is the correct choice. It is fast and safe because the length enables you to reach the snow without stooping and the less steeply angled pick is easier to use when ice axe breaking.

The named components in the photograph on page 60 each have a separate function:

ADZE – is used mainly for cutting and clearing snow or for chipping away ice. It can be used for insertion into snow when ice axe breaking in soft snow – where its greater area offers more resistance than a pick. Or conversely it can be inserted into tougher snow when the snow is supportive (névé).

PICK – this is the most used point of contact with the snow or ice and is driven into the snow or ice for pulling on or ice axe breaking.

SPIKE – another important feature to secure the climber on snow or ice.

SHAFT – should have a bonded rubber section to help the grip and absorb the impact shock. Most high tech shafts are of alloy.

EYE FOR CRAB OR TAPE – essential at the head of the axe to take the wrist loop but also useful near or in the spike to clip for taking belay load. (Note: check this is large enough to clip a Crab and strong enough to take the load!)

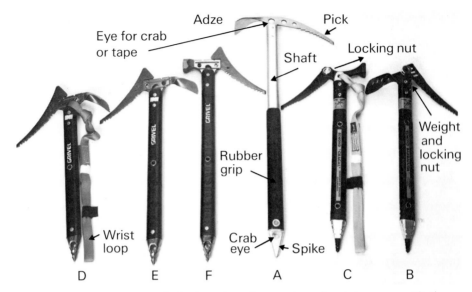

A selection of modern axes for both moderately steep (snow) and steep ground (ice).
(A) 65cm axe – Mountain Technology   (D) 45cm axe – Grivel
(B) 50cm – Simond Barracuda   (E) 50cm axe – Grivel
(C) 50cm hammer – Simond Chacal   (F) 55cm hammer – Grivel

WRIST LOOP – must be positioned as shown, secured at the head and threaded around the adze/hammer side of the axe. It is positioned thus because this is the correct balance point through which to load the axe and it is on the opposite side of the shaft to the pick so that the tape will not suffer impact damage when the pick is swung home. If you're as clumsy as I am, and frequently bang the ice and protruding rock with your knuckles, then this is an important point. A further vital detail is to get the wrist loop correctly dimensioned to take the gloved/mitted hand:

(1) It must be of the right length (when the hand is inserted in the loop) to bear the climber's weight when the hand is positioned gripping the bottom of the shaft (just above the spike). This gives the climber full swinging power to drive the pick home.

(2) The actual loop must be of sufficient size to allow the gloved hand to be easily inserted and withdrawn yet still supportive enough to take the load when climbing. (The wrist loops illustrated are adjustable.)

A further consideration is the retrieval of the axe, on steep ice, when it has been dropped purposely to suspend from the wrist loops (perhaps when using an odd rock handhold). It can be quite difficult to regain grip on the shaft, one-handed, when it dangles with shaft hanging vertically, down below. One answer to this is to tape the wrist loop to the shaft, so changing the point of balance of the dangling axe and allowing the shaft to rotate easily back into the hand when required – as in the diagram on page 61.

WEIGHTS AND LOCKING NUTS – most modern tools have a facility for replacing the pick in the event of breakage (or for fitting picks of alternate design) and some have removable weights to change the swing characteristics of the axe.

Taping the wrist loop to the shaft of the axe for easy retrieval. The suspension point is still the head of the axe, but insulating tape holds the wrist loop to the shaft and allows freedom of movement but facilitates easy retrieval of the dangling axe simply by changing the point of balance.

LONG AXE

(A) illustrates a long axe (65cm) suitable for single axe techniques on moderately steep ground. Even though the pick is of the dropped curve shape, toothed to improve the grip, and is superb for gripping in névé it is unsuitable for steep ice. (The curved shape by design pivots out of the ice, and the ice supporting the weight simultaneously acts as a fulcrum.)

ICE TOOLS

(B) illustrates an axe, with adze, suitable for steep ice. Note the design of pick which is a reverse curve, known as the "elephant's trunk" or "banana" shape. This configuration of pick is probably the best overall for climbing steep technical ground. An alternative design of pick is a hollow tube which is perhaps superior on steep brittle water ice but which blunts and deforms, rendering it useless, if rock is struck. As most British routes involve mixed ground the tubular pick is not really a practical choice.

(C) illustrates an ice hammer, an axe on which the hammer head replaces the adze. This is used for placing rock and ice pegs (drive-in type).

(B) & (C) are a matched pair suitable for front pointing.

Length Considerations

(D), (E) and (F) are ice tools, for steep ground, of 45cm, 50cm and 55cm length respectively. The shorter tool is suitable for use in confined spaces – gullies. The mid size is the best for climbers of average build, allowing a good hefty swing at the ice and offering an effective reach. For those with strong arms and elongated stature the longest may well be the wisest choice.

Use

Full use is discussed under "Techniques" but, as a general comment here, make positive placement in the ice with a good swing, clearing away brittle or rotten ice as necessary. The illustrated picks grip well and extraction can be a problem. As a general tip do not move too high on placed axes (tools), but it is only practice that will give you the skill to climb without this becoming a problem.

Both the spike and the pick are used to place ice screws, depending on the amount of required leverage and the amount of clearance available for free rotation of the shaft.

Care

Be watchful for cracks or other signs of failure and never attempt to modify structurally axes of any description. With the steels now in use when sharpening is required it should only be done with a hand file, and done in moderation. Razor sharp tools will quickly blunt and the temptation to oversharpen should be resisted. Regularly inspect the wrist loop, checking for damage and making sure that any knot is tight and sound.

BOOTS AND CRAMPONS

Gone are the days of cramming cold feet into leather boots literally frozen solid from the previous day's adventures. Sometimes the feet never seemed to thaw out; the leather boots eventually did, of course, but then let even more water through to the feet. I remember, too, how the flanks of the Ben were strewn with snapped, so-called unbreakable, crampon tying straps. Thankfully equipment now available is more comfortable, reliable and safer.

Each component in the photograph opposite has a separate function: BASE POINTS – these are used when flatfooting or travelling over ground of moderate steepness. Modern crampons (with the exception of Footfangs which have more) have ten base points.

FRONT POINTS – the crucial points used in the front pointing technique. Generally, most crampons have two and these should stick out in front of the boot by ½" to ¾" (13mm to 20mm).

TOE BAR/BAIL – this clips over the front welt (ledge above the sole) to hold the crampon on.

HEEL CLAMP – this pivots onto the back welt to tighten and hold the crampon on the boot.

SECURITY STRAP – once the heel is clamped and secure the actual clamp is retained in the vertical section by the security strap.

RUBBER RAND – this promotes friction when the plastic boot is used in a rock climbing situation.

INNER BOOT – fits inside the outer plastic shell and provides comfort and warmth. Different grades are available for different degrees of cold.

PLASTIC BOOTS

These are light, comfortable, waterproof and warm (even at altitude in winter – with the right choice of inner boots) and do not freeze solid. They are suitable for all snow and ice work and for approach and mountain rock climbing. They are sufficiently stiff to support steep continuous cramponing (front pointing) and yet are light and sensitive enough to be suitable for walking to approach an ice climb.

(A) illustrates a pair of plastic boots suitable for all types of ice climbing and winter mountaineering. In construction they have a rubber (Vibram type) sole mounted onto a waterproof plastic shell, inside of which goes an inner boot designed to provide comfort and warmth. This inner boot can be selected to suit the conditions and environment in which the climber chooses to execute his craft, be it the north face of Ben Nevis in winter or at altitude in the Himalayas.

Care

Air drying, stuffing inner boots with newspaper overnight (not really appropriate whilst actually on the north face of the Eiger), away from direct heat sources, and sympathetic storage when not in use is all the maintenance that is required.

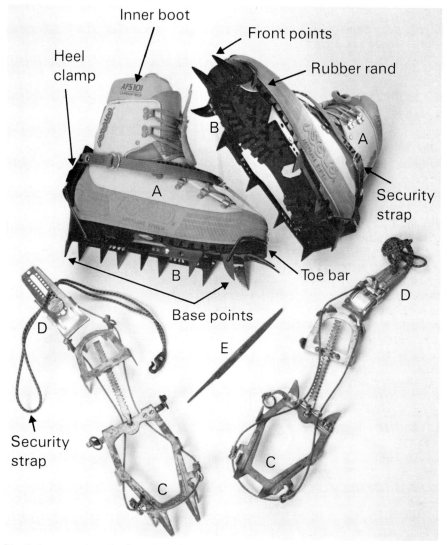

Plastic boots and a selection of crampons.
(A) Plastic boots
(B) Step-in, rigid and adjustable crampons
(C) Adjustable articulated crampons
(D) Cable bindings
(E) Sharpening file.

CRAMPONS AND BINDINGS

The best type of modern crampon has its own integral system to fasten to the boot.

(B) (p. 63) illustrates a pair of Grivel crampons which combine a number of important features. They fit easily and securely to the boot, utilising a simple but effective and safe *step-in* system of fastening to the boot. They give a *rigid* platform for the boot, which supports the load of front pointing, yet they are easily *adjustable* to fit different boot sizes.

(C) illustrates a pair of adjustable articulated crampons. These are more flexible than rigid crampons and some climbers prefer this type when mixed ground (snow and rock) is to be climbed or travelled over. They are suitable for modern front pointing when placed on plastic boots because the boots themselves are rigid enough to take the loading induced.

It will be seen that these crampons are designed to take the old style tape bindings, with six rings, but that the securing system used is a Cable Binding (D) which makes the fastening and unfastening of the crampons onto the boot much quicker and easier. Used correctly this is a secure system and is a reasonable method (Cable Bindings can be purchased separately in three different sizes) of modifying old style crampons.

Use

Flatfooting and front pointing are explained in "Techniques" but a general point that should be emphasised here is that all crampon placements should be made positively and firmly. Unless on the thinnest of ice, put them in with some force.

Care

Check visually for damage after every day out.

(E) illustrates a typical sharpening file but, like the ice axe made from modern steels, sharpening of crampons is not as important today as it used to be. Really there is absolutely no need to have crampon points razor sharp and, in fact, this is detrimental because when the inevitable rocky ground is reached points so sharpened will quickly blunt and even distort under the point loading they will receive.

If and when sharpening is necessary, it must be done by hand (*never grind, as this destroys the temper*) and done correctly as detailed in the diagram, otherwise the crampons will be ruined.

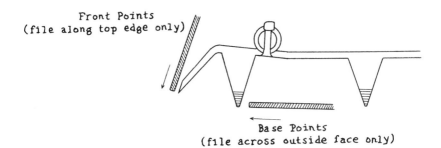

Sharpening crampons. The correct procedure for sharpening points is to file across the greater face of the points (so maintaining the strength of each point). Any sharpening must be done in moderation; razor sharp points are not desirable.

ICE CLIMBING GEAR

The following photograph illustrates some important items of equipment for the ice climber and winter mountaineer.

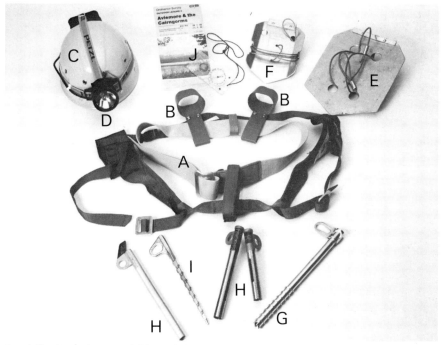

Specialised gear is essential for safe ice climbing and winter mountaineering.

(A) Harness	(F) Deadboy snow runner plate
(B) Axe holsters	(G) Chouinard tubular screw-in ice screw
(C) Helmet	(H) Snargs, tubular drive in-screw out ice screws
(D) Headtorch	(I) Drive in-screw out ice screw
(E) Deadman snow anchor plate	(J) Map and compass

HARNESS

(A) illustrates a harness suitable for the ice climber. Note carefully the opening leg loops and lack of padding on the waist belt. Note: a *Whillans Harness* does not require the leg loops to be opened and rebuckled and is the simplest harness, with sit and waist support, to fit over winter clothing.

AXE HOLSTERS

(B) illustrates axe holsters which are extremely important for carrying short axes when on steep ground. The solid plastic type allow easy, trouble-free withdrawal and replacement.

CLIMBING HELMET

(C) illustrates the helmet which I consider to be an essential part of the ice climber's equipment when on or near steep ground. I have been knocked out twice by falling ice (and once by a falling rock – but that's another story) and on the second occasion the helmet probably saved my life.

Check out the lightness and comfort and the fastenings and webbing, and make sure it has UIAA approval. Also, look to see that it has suitable fastening points for securing the head torch.

HEAD TORCH

(D) illustrates a head torch and this should be considered to be a vital piece of survival equipment during the short daylight hours of winter. The best type have the battery positioned at the back and the lens at the front. Carry a spare bulb and ensure the battery has ample life: they have a bad habit of deteriorating in cold conditions, even when not used.

ANCHOR PLATES

(E) and (F) illustrate the *deadman* and *deadboy* anchor plates respectively. Fixed correctly (and this is essential to prevent them pulling out), these plates are the best anchors to be taken in snow. The deadboy is smaller and easier to carry but does not offer the same holding capacity as the deadman, which is the one to be used in a full anchor situation.

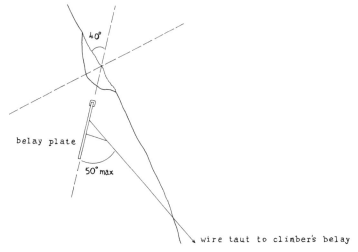

Fixing deadman/deadboy snow anchor plates. Correct placing is essential: insert plates at 40 degrees to the slope. First dig away soft snow, then drive home the plate with the hammer.

ICE SCREWS

The various types have different properties and all these should be carefully assessed and then the choice of screw made for the prevailing conditions. Different lengths are available; decision about length should be based on the expected depth of ice to be encountered. It is much better and more secure to place a screw with the eye tight against the ice than to have it sticking proud (because it has bottomed on rock) and tied off.

(G) illustrates the *hollow tubular screw in–screw out* type and this is the most secure of all the different types of ice screw. The modern Chouinard type illustrated here is tapered to facilitate ice extraction once the screw has been withdrawn and, theoretically, the ice should clear (it needs to be hollow and ice free to be re-used) with a good bang from the ice axe. In practice it often requires cleaning out with a length of wire.

In good ice these screws offer a reasonable degree of security and for the experienced climber they are the easiest type of screw to place on vertical ice (see "Techniques"). Most prefer to use axe pick or spike to place this type of screw, although a specially made ratchet is available. For the ice climbing millionaire these are available in titanium and are exceptionally light.

(H) illustrates *Snargs* which are hollow drive in–screw out screws. These are second best to tubular screw ins in holding power. They are hammered into place and screwed out to remove; a slot in the side of the tube allows the ice to be scraped out with the pick, so facilitating their re-use. The two grouped together here are titanium and the single is light aluminium alloy.

(I) illustrates the solid drive in–screw out type and this gives very little holding power unless placed into a fairly horizontal section of ice, i.e. into a ledge or large ice boss, with the shaft vertical. It is, for the inexperienced, the easiest type of screw to place when in a comfortable standing position on moderately steep ground (it usually requires the use of both hands to get started – try doing that on vertical ice!) Being solid, it does not require the ice to be removed after extraction and so the screw is the most problem-free to re-use.

Placing

For more detailed comment see "Techniques", but generally the screw should be placed at right angles to the ice and "starred" (radial fracture lines) or "dinner plated" (concave fracture planes) or shattered ice should be cleared away. First, a starter hole should be made with the pick and then (with the screw-in type) the screw should be inserted as far as possible with the hand. The screw should be taken in until the eye is tight against the ice where possible and, if protruding, it must be tied off to reduce the leverage.

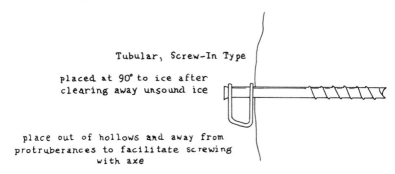

Tubular, Screw-In Type

placed at 90° to ice after
clearing away unsound ice

place out of hollows and away from
protruberances to facilitate screwing
with axe

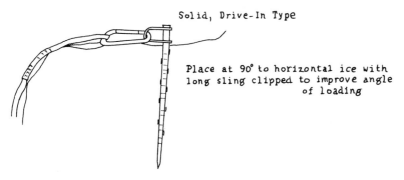

Solid, Drive-In Type

Place at 90° to horizontal ice with
long sling clipped to improve angle
of loading

Positioning of an ice screw. Positioning is an important consideration in both holding power and ease of placement and extraction.

Rotation with the axe. The screw is positioned to allow free rotation of the axe, with either the pick or the spike inserted into the eye of the screw.

MAP AND COMPASS

These are essential to safety in winter mountaineering, along with the ability to navigate (see "Safety").

THERMOMETER

Small plastic thermometers are available to clip onto the sac and these are a very useful aid in assessing the prevailing ice conditions.

SLEEPING BAGS

The type wholly depends on use. The main choices are Gortex Outer, Down or Synthetic-filled. Synthetic-filled resist water penetration but are heavier and bulkier to carry; they also tend to compress with frequent use and lose some of their insulating properties. Before you go to the shop decide exactly what you want the bag to do and then choose accordingly.

BIVVI BAGS

Those made from Gortex (or similar function material) are the most suitable for planned bivouacs but the carrying of cheap and light polythene bags for emergencey use is worth considering.

MOUNTAIN WINTER CLOTHING

Winter snow and ice conditions can be extreme. To survive them in good health and to remain frost bite free it is necessary to adopt the correct survival technique. An essential part of this technique, and a vital component in climbing performance, is the right choice and wearing of specialist mountain winter clothing. The climber needs to stay as light and flexible as possible whilst maintaining comfort and survival potential, i.e. whilst remaining dry and maintaining the right body (and digit) temperature.

Winter snow and ice climbing consist of a number of quite different activities: the approach and climbing require high energy output, yet there are occasions, sometimes protracted, when the climber is virtually stationary (when belaying or resting, for example). Take the variance in the winter weather as a further function in the equation, varying from hot sunshine in clear blue skies to a howling blizzard, and it can be seen that the selection of correct clothing requires some careful consideration.

With modern clothing and materials the ice climber can achieve a high degree of comfort and survival potential. However it requires correct selection and combination, based on sound principles of function and performance. The concept of layering enables the climber to select a range of gear which he combines, i.e. takes on or off, as conditions dictate.

Firstly, there is the bottom layer of undergarments which keep the climber warm and dry. They contain heat, yet allow the dispersion of perspiration. Then there is the second layer which gives extra warmth and possible protection against the prevailing elements. The third layer is the outer protective shell which protects the climber from the natural elements of wind, rain or snow.

We will now look at the available clothing combinations in detail, but remember: the golden rules are keep warm and dry, have spare clothing available if required (a light pullover in the sac, for example) and keep clothing as light and flexible as possible.

FIRST LAYER

This layer usually stays on the climber throughout the trip and is designed to keep the climber warm and dry by allowing the passage of perspiration but the retention of heat.

In the photograph on page 70, (A) illustrates a polyester-based balaclava style helmet. It is most often used in a bivouac situation and is kept in the Sac, but it could be used under the climbing helmet.

(B) & (C) illustrate polyester or polypropolene vest and "long johns" respectively.

(D) illustrates short socks that may be used under woollen socks to soak up sweat or as a spare if outer socks become sodden.

(E) shows long wool/nylon loop socks which offer warmth and durability.

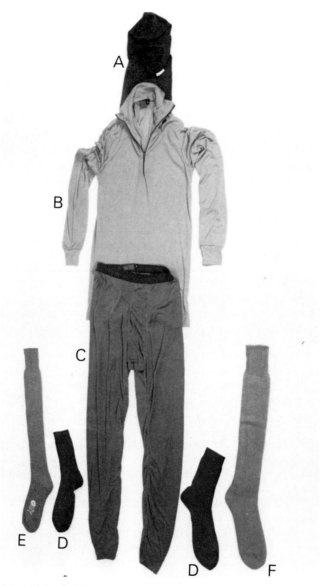

First layer clothing. This clothing remains in place whilst a climber is in the mountain environment.

SECOND LAYER

Some items stay in place permanently, whilst others are worn as conditions dictate.

In the photograph on page 71, (A) illustrates the traditional woollen balaclava on the right and a fibre pile alternative on the left. Wool may be a bit ticklish, but its heat retention and snow resisting qualities are well proved. Keeping the head warm is exceptionally important to the climber, for heat loss through the head is quite considerable. If the head is left unprotected, energy will be lost and the body temperature will be lowered.

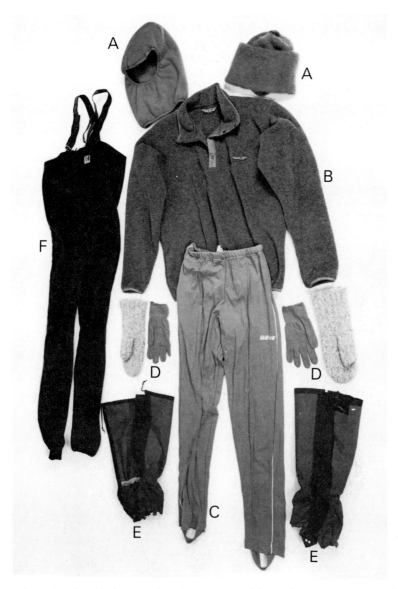

Second layer clothing. Various combinations are possible and items are worn to suit the prevailing conditions.

(B) illustrates a fibre pile top. Warm and light, this sort of top is a good climbing garment and can be worn as the last layer (as a jacket), but be warned: they are neither waterproof nor windproof. I prefer a full length zip to regulate heat loss whilst the jacket is in place. An alternative here would be a woollen pullover, although it is bulkier and heavier.

(C) illustrates nylon tracksuit bottoms which, combined with the "long johns" provide a light and flexible bottom body combination. They are both warm (as a combination) and dry quickly. They stay on the whole time (with obvious exceptions not to be detailed here!) and often suffice to provide the outer shell.

71

(D) illustrates the winter climber's handwear. These are imperative to prevent frost bite and to keep the fingers working and comfortable. Always wear both inner gloves (thin and flexible) and outer mitts when climbing. The outer mitts illustrated are wool and in my experience, for a number of reasons, I have found these preferable to the alternatives. However others prefer the lighter weight and greater sensitivity of suitably lined nylon gloves and these dry out quicker too. Whatever your choice it is very important that the climber does not have to manage without gloves and as a precaution against dropping the outer mitts it is useful to sew to them an elastic cord that loops around the wrist. A wise precaution is to carry a spare pair in the sac. Wool socks will do the job if you haven't got a spare pair.

(E) illustrates the gaiter, another feature that can provide an outer shell, and this is vital to keep the snow/slush/mud (moving from the Scottish myth to the oft reality!) off the leg and out of the boots. Gaiters come in all shapes, sizes, materials and designs, but I find the simple front-zipping type illustrated here to be the most practically functional.

(F) illustrates the fibre pile salopette which has no mid-waist break and therefore can be a useful means of heat retention. It is a worthwhile alternative if you intend to linger in low temperatures or extremely cold conditions. There are both obvious advantages and disadvantages with the salopette and I will leave it to the individual to decide on its worth for the particular occasion.

THE OUTER SHELL

The outer layer is all important to keep the climber warm and dry in wind, rain, sleet or snow or any combination of these. To do this it must serve two main separate functions, that is, both to keep the elements out and to let away the damp body vapours (sweat) and excess heat. It is a tall order but it is performed admirably by Gortex (and similar performing materials), and a number of garments are manufactured from this remarkable material. However, let it be said that nothing is perfect and Gortex (and its alternatives) does have limitations. This must be remembered whilst considering its application out in the field.

I personally have never found a garment that is 100% waterproof and breathable in all conditions, despite claims to the contrary, so use your own discretion. There are many different qualities that affect the performance of a particular garment and the subject would fill a book on its own. So, as a piece of general advice, go to a reputable shop, ask questions and buy a product from a manufacturer that has a reputation to protect. Look at the standard of construction and find out whether the seams are taped or welded; compare prices and make your own decision.

In the photograph on page 73, (A) illustrates a Gortex jacket (note: there are different layers and plies of gortex available, offering different qualities, and these should be discussed in the shop before purchase) with a number of features that should be sought after. The pockets are well placed and sized, and are protected with both flap and zip. The garment length is suitable to extend below the midriff gap. It zips and fastens shut to keep even the finest driving spindrift out. The sleeve collars are velcroed to allow adjustable tight fastening, preventing ingress of snow which is especially important when the hands are above the head in snow gullies. It has a substantial collar to turn and keep out wind and anything blown by it! The hood is large enough to fit over the climbing helmet, keeping out the

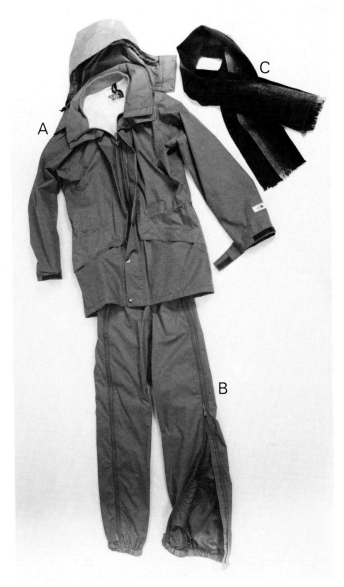

The outer layer. This should both protect a climber from the elements and also allow his body to breathe, i.e. it should prevent water ingress and should form an effective barrier against the wind, but it should allow dispersal of wetting body vapour.

spindrift avalanches, and to allow unrestricted movement of the head – enabling a look down at the second relaxing on his stance 100ft below, a look up to the overhanging ice above and a look around to the tourists strolling up the easy way! The hood rim is also wired to maintain profile and eyeview, and has a draw cord to fasten the inner section tight to protect the whole face.

(C) illustrates a scarf. This is necessary to keep fine snow from

73

penetrating the neck area (if you haven't got a jacket with all the protective features like the one above).

(B) illustrates Gortex "over trousers". Note the full length leg zips, which allows quick and easy placement over climbing boots and crampons. Ensure that these zips are both free running and robust. An alternative to over trousers, which stop at the waist, are Gortex salopettes. Supported by braces, these extend to the high chest. Salopettes are good to prevent the ingress of snow in the event of a backside slide (planned or unplanned) but you need to take the jacket off to position the braces.

THE MOUNTAIN WINTER APPROACH

Most of the important points have already been covered (see also Chapter 2), but it is worth having a look at the assembled equipment.

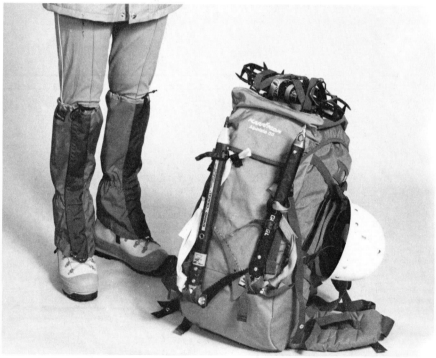

Sac packed ready to go.

The climber has utilised the external gear loops and has placed outside those items of equipment that are sharp/awkward to place inside and which will not be adversely affected if they are snowed on. Check that your winter sac has these facilities and that they do actually work! (There are sacs available on which the loops just do not work in practice.) This system allows the maximum space in the sac for dry clothing, etc. Personally, I try to get all my equipment in the sac and one useful trick to achieve this without damage is to fold (articulated type only) the crampon points inwards and place them inside the helmet. Another important tip is to place dry clothing inside a polythene bag, inside the sac, hence keeping it dry however severe the conditions.

The climber here is approaching in dry conditions and he is simply wearing gaiters over his tracksuit bottoms and boots.

It is very easy when going hard on the approach to get cold hands and fingers without knowing it until it is too late. It's better to have gloves on if there is any doubt about this and in any case if there is any scrambling through snow, where the hands come into contact with the snow, ensure that the mitts are on before contact is made – otherwise feeling and circulation are lost very quickly.

Another method of carrying the ice axe, for quick access in case it is required, is to tuck it, spike down, between sac and back, with the shaft in a diagonal position. The spike sticks out at the side and the head rests on the top of the sac where it can be reached with the hand over the shoulder. Alternatively, it can be tucked into the sac waist belt, although it tends to get in the way there.

Dressed for the approach (2).
Dave has shouldered his sac and is on his way. Because of the strong, cold wind, he's wearing his Gortex jacket, balaclava helmet and is donning his undergloves. It's a long walk-in and it's steep. Energy output is going to be high; to prevent overheating and wetting with sweat, Dave wears simply an under vest (polyester or polypropylene) and keeps the jacket zip down for ventilation. If the wind increases or the temperature drops with increasing altitude, he can adjust the zip.

Lead climber ready to go. Tied on to double ropes, making a final adjustment to his gear, Dave is now ready and equipped to climb a mixed route involving steep ice with some rock and snow.

LEAD CLIMBER READY TO GO ON ICE

For more detailed observations see the diagram on page 76. Here it can be seen that the climber has his helmet on and his sac is on his back. Both are important on winter routes. Even on short routes it is sound practice to carry all spare equipment, etc., because returning to the bottom of the climb can become a severe and dangerous undertaking in winter conditions, especially if the weather unexpectedly deteriorates.

The climber has an axe in one hand, wrist loop in position, and the other he will pull from the holster when he finishes racking his gear. Note that the rack consists of a varied mixture of rock and ice protection, balanced for the route he is about to undertake. He is carrying four ice screws and it is very seldom that a climber would carry more than this because of the strenuosity involved in placing them.

Remember in chapter 2 how it was explained how to clip on the long slings (ends clipped together) so they pull through without having to be lifted over the head. Long slings, in addition to tie-offs, are important in winter.

Well, we could wish Dave luck before he sets off, but really there is no need – he relies on his climbing ability (technical competence in addition to rope management skill) and good judgement (based on a sound understanding of his climbing environment and the prevailing conditions) to succeed. Let's just say, "Have a good climb lad!"

4
ROPE
TECHNIQUES

There are old climbers and there are bold climbers, but there are no old, bold climbers. Well, there are a few actually, but effective use and knowledge of modern rope techniques, coupled with correct rope management, are second nature to all good climbers and the ability to master rope management is a matter of pride. There is also a distinct fringe benefit that you, as a careful climber, can reasonably expect to live longer than a careless climber.

Climbing is, of course, a spectacular and exciting sport but within this image is the fact that it should and can be a safe activity. Self-preservation is a basic human instinct and correct rope techniques and management are fundamental to climbing safety. Note carefully, too, when you climb as a unit, that you as an individual are responsible for the safety not only of yourself but of all members of the team.

Rope is used to safeguard all members of the climbing party and this is true for the many different forms of the sport (even soloing!). As climbing, along with the equipment used by climbers, has developed so have the techniques and different systems of rope management. Today each branch of the sport (rock climbing, snow and ice climbing and mountaineering, for example) have developed their own particular specialist systems and the most modern and best of these will all be explained in this chapter. However, importantly, the basic concept of all rope management is fundamentally the same – that of protecting the climbing party.

Effective rope management is essential for safety.

So, firstly, I will explain the basic principles of ropework in the climbing team and then I will detail the component parts: the knots, rope management and belaying. Other essential techniques include descending (abseiling) and ascending (prusiking) fixed rope and these will be dealt with before looking into the rope and protection techniques for both rock and ice climbing.

BASIC ROPE TECHNIQUE

The general principles of this are simple to grasp, are essential to adhere to and are best illustrated in their progressive stages.

2nd man

Leader

Screwgate crab

Belay plate

Figure of eight knot

Gear racked ready to climb

Leader – tied on with figure of eight (and stopper) knot

Rope laid to be tangle free

Belay anchor (for upward pull)

Commencing a climb.

LEADER SAYS – (when all are tied on, 2nd is belayed and leader has all his gear and is ready to climb) – *"Climbing"*.
2ND SAYS – (when he has the leader belayed): *"OK!"*
Comment: Only on receipt of the "OK" from the 2nd does the leader start climbing.

Leader clips rope into runner

2nd man feeds leader sufficient rope to clip the runner

Leader places a runner.

LEADER SAYS – (when the runner is placed and the rope is clipped through the crab, i.e. only when the runner is an effective unit): *"Runner clipped!"*
2ND SAYS – *"OK!"*

Comment: The leader is now safeguarded in the event of a fall. Note the following illustration showing what will happen in the event of a fall.

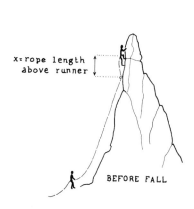

x = rope length above runner

BEFORE FALL

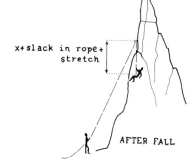

x + slack in rope + stretch

AFTER FALL

Note:
total fall distance = 2x + slack + stretch

Leader falling onto a runner.　　　Leader arrives at stance and belays self.

Procedure: Leader arrives at a suitable stance and belay point (usually at the end of a rope length) and makes himself secure.
LEADER SAYS – (when the belay is on): *"I'm safe!"*
2ND SAYS – *"OK – taking you off!"*
Comment: Only when the leader is safely belayed does the 2nd take him off the belay. A free-running rope is easier for the leader to take in, which is the next stage. However, if leader and 2nd at this stage are out of sight and out of hearing (as is often the case), and communication is impossible, then the 2nd should not take the leader off belay unless certain the leader is secure.

Leader takes in the rope.   Leader belays the 2nd.

Procedure: Leader takes in the slack rope, until it is tight, directly to the second man. This includes taking in the slack rope that formed the knot, etc. of the 2nd's belay.

2ND SAYS – "*That's me*!" (Alternatively, if the rope remains slack, 2nd says "Take in!")

LEADER SAYS – (when he has put the 2nd on belay): "*Climb when you are ready*".

2ND SAYS – (only when actually starting to climb): "*Climbing*!"

Procedure: The 2nd stops climbing and takes runners out and clips them to his/her harness. Leader stops taking in the rope and avoids pulling the 2nd off balance as he removes the equipment.

2nd removes runners.

2ND SAYS – *"Taking off runner!"*
LEADER SAYS – *"OK"*
Comment: This is an important stage in the sequence, as a "stuck" runner can take some time to remove. To prevent "fraying of tempers" and jerking/pulling of the rope by the leader (to determine if it is jammed) he needs to know what exactly the 2nd is doing.

83

2nd man clips to anchors

before leader takes him off belay plate

2nd arrives at stance.

At this stage it is vital that the 2nd man is tied on to a belay and that he in turn belays the leader before the leader commences to climb the next pitch. (Alternatively, if the 2nd goes on to lead through on the next pitch he must be tied on whilst the gear (runners) are transferred or if another member of the party follows up the pitch below.) At no stage should leader and second be untied or off belay simultaneously. In practice, on a hanging stance where there is no ledge or footholds, this requires a planned sequence of weight transfer, usually involving two or more belay points. (This will be explained in detail later.)

This sequence of basic rope technique (of which the individual components and terminologies of belaying and rope management will be explained fully in the following text) is essential to safe climbing. The language and actions may seem simplistic, but it is vital to stick precisely and methodically to this basic sequence. Later, when a few easier climbs have been achieved, more difficult and perhaps much longer climbs will be done. If on these climbs the weather turns from good to bad, fatigue takes its toll and overhangs prevent both visual and verbal communication, it is the above disciplined regime that will keep you safe.

THE KNOTS

The starting point needed to effect the rope mechanics in all rope techniques is most obviously the joining factor: the knot. Humble they may be, but climbing knots support life and they are vital to a climber's survival: they should be learned well.

Of all the many knots that can be tied there are only a few simple ones that are needed by the climber. The following section illustrates fully and comprehensively the knots required in all facets of the climbing game. These fulfil the arduous requirements of a climbing knot. Although there are other climbing knots that can be tied, it is better to know those mentioned here to a point at which they become second nature and can be tied intuitively than to have knowledge of others that are, in reality, superfluous to the practical situation.

An important general point which applies to all these knots is that of tightening. After tying they must all be worked tight and carefully inspected to see that they look and "lie" correctly. Finally, the free ends of the knot must be pulled tight, the knot bedded-in, and the main knot finished with a stopper knot or insulating (binding) tape as indicated. The stopper knots most used in practice are a double half-hitch or a single half-hitch (a single is used only when fastened on either side of the main knot, i.e. used twice).

The following text describes each knot, specifies their uses and comments on the relative merits of each. Observation of the photograph sequences will enable you to tie each knot stage by stage. Practise them thoroughly and remember, in the mind's eye, just what the completed knot looks like – if this is done, mistakes will be avoided on the hills.

BOWLINE

(To be used in conjunction with a stopper knot.)

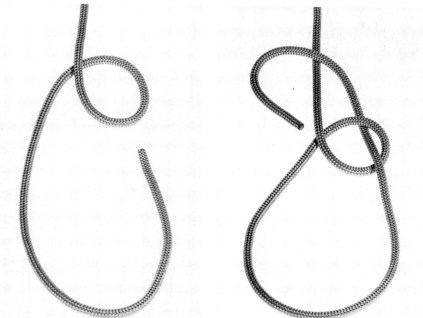

Bowline (and half hitch), stage 1.   Stage 2.

85

Stage 3.

Complete (tightened) bowline with half stopper knot. (To be tightened and repeated on the lead rope, or doubled.)

Uses: The Bowline is the traditional tying-on knot. It is used to tie the ends of the main rope to a harness (originally tied directly around the waist) or to fix a rope around a thread, tree or natural belay.

Comment: Tied alone in modern kermantel ropes, this knot can loosen and come undone. It is, therefore, *essential* that the bowline is backed up with a *stopper knot*, such as a *half-hitch*. It is, however, a strong and simple knot that can be adjusted easily.

FIGURE OF EIGHT

(Stopper knot advised.)

Uses: It can be tied in three separate ways, all with different uses, as described here. Tied in its threaded form at the end of the rope it is used for tying into the harness. Or it can be tied by taking a loop at any point along the length of a rope and here the figure of eight can be clipped to a Crab and used for belaying or to tie a middle man to the rope. It can also be used to tie two ropes together for abseiling.

Comment: This versatile knot is the strongest knot of all for tying onto or to clip into and, once tied, it does not tend to work loose, although a stopper knot is a worthwhile precaution. Used for these purposes its minor disadvatages are that it may be difficult to untie after a fall and that it is difficult to adjust. It is an easy knot to recognise and even if tied incorrectly it turns into an Overhand Knot.

It is an excellent knot to join two main ropes for abseiling, because it is safe, is easily identifiable, presents a "flat face" enabling the ropes to be pulled without snagging, and (in this form) undoes easily. The last two points are two major advantages over any other knot, particularly in a mountain situation where time and rope recovery can be important factors in survival. All in all then, the figure of eight, in these three forms, is an extremely valuable knot to the climber.

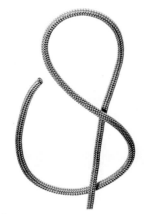

Figure of eight – threaded for tieing on, stage 1.

Stage 2.

Stage 3.

Stage 4.

Complete (but untightened) figure of eight.

Figure of eight (mid-rope) – for belaying to crab, stage 1.

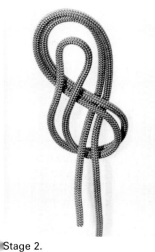

Stage 2.

Completed (tightened) figure of eight.

Joining two main ropes with figure of eight – for abseiling, stage 1.

87

Stage 2.   Completed (tightened) joining figure of eight.

OVERHAND KNOT

Uses: To clip a crab when belaying, but not to be used for tying on a climber.

Comments: This knot is quick and simple to tie, does not tend to work undone and so has attractions for belaying leader or second to a crab. Really, it is a poor man's version of the figure of eight and does not have the strength of the latter – therefore, it should not be used for tying on.

Overhand – to clip crab, stage 1.   Completed overhand knot (untightened).

CLOVE HITCH

Uses: To clip a crab when belaying.

Comment: Fast and simple to tie, it is a popular knot to clip a crab when belaying. It is relatively low on strength (compared with the figure of eight or the overhand) and is easy to get wrong, despite its simplicity. Practise this knot until its correct, finished form is instantly recognisable.

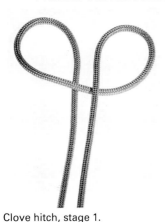

Clove hitch, stage 1.   Stage 2.   Completed (tightened) clove hitch.

LARK'S FOOT

Uses: For "tying off" pegs with thin line or tape.

Comment: This is a basic knot used for tying off pegs that cannot be fully driven home. It is vital to reduce the load (bending moment or lever) on a peg that cannot be fully bedded home and in an extreme free climbing situation it needs to be done quickly and ideally one-handed. This simple little knot fulfils all these requirements. Ensure the knot is pushed as close to the rock as possible and that it is tightened sufficiently to prevent it lifting off the peg. Thin tape is best used, as this bites when tightened. Practise tying the knot with a sling taken from around the neck and held in free space with one hand only.

Lark's foot, stage 1.   Stage 2.   Completed (tightened) lark's foot.

ITALIAN HITCH

Uses: It provides a quick method of belaying the second or lead climber.
Comments: A traditional knot used extensively before the invention of the Sticht Plate system of belaying. It still has its place when used in an Alpine or mountaineering situation or on ground of moderate steepness. Here it provides a belaying system that is easy (once learned) and quick to apply. A falling second can be stopped without undue difficulty, if there is no slack in the rope, and it is also possible to halt a minor leader fall. However, there are serious disadvantages in this system of belaying. Firstly, it directly loads the belay anchor without the valuable and energy-absorbing "cushioning" provided by the weight of the belayer's body and elasticity of harness, etc. This means the belay stands a greater chance of failure. Secondly, although the knot is simplicity in itself, it is very easy to get this knot wrong – with the obvious consequences. Experience will dictate the time to use this knot, but suffice to say here that I very rarely foresake the foolproof belay plate (Sticht Plate or other) system of belaying for this knot.

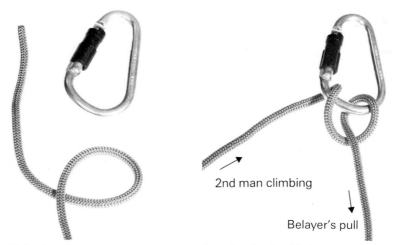

2nd man climbing

Belayer's pull

Italian hitch, stage 1.   Completed Italian hitch.
Note: this knot automatically pulls through and reverses, depending on the direction of pull on the rope. The illustrated position of tying is correct for all situations.

SINGLE FISHERMAN'S KNOT

(To be used only with free ends bound with insulating tape.)

Uses: Joining line slings up to 5mm in diameter. (Line greater than 5mm will not allow the knot to bite when tightened and in these cases the knot should not be used.)

Single fisherman's knot, stage 1.

Stage 2.

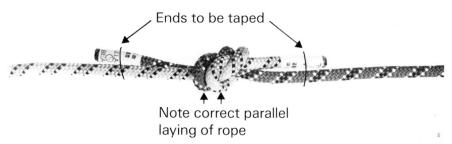

Ends to be taped

Note correct parallel
laying of rope

Completed (tightened) single fisherman's knot.

Comment: This knot can work loose and should only be used in fine line (suggested maximum diameter 5mm) with the free ends taped (free ends and sling body are wrapped around with insulating tape). It should not be used for any component that is going to take climbing loading. This limits it to cosmetic jobs, such as forming the carrying loop on a Sticht Plate.

DOUBLE FISHERMAN'S KNOT

(Taping of the ends when forming permanent slings is recommended.)

Uses: To join two main ropes for abseiling or for forming line slings.

Comment: This is one of the strongest knots of all for joining rope and is reassuringly solid under load. It requires attention to tie correctly and it must be carefully checked so that, when tied, the four coils lie snug and parallel to each other. It is quite difficult to untie once load has been applied, but there is a specific method, that of flipping the inner coils over the outer coils as illustrated, which makes it easier. Another disadvantage is the chunky nature of the knot which can be a problem with snagging when pulling down an abseil rope. For abseiling purposes (joining two main ropes) this knot has been somewhat superseded by the figure of eight.

Double fisherman's knot, stage 1.

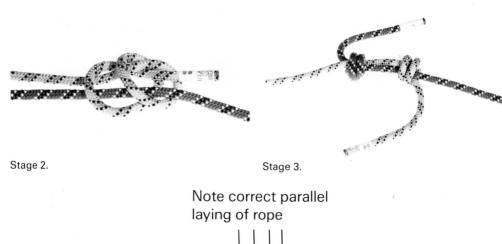

Stage 2.   Stage 3.

Note correct parallel
laying of rope

Tape ends when used
in permanent rope sling

Completed (tightened) double fisherman's knot.

Thumb
pulls over
inside loop

Undoing double fisherman's knot, stage 1.   Stage 2.

TAPE KNOT
(To be used only when free ends are bound to main sling with insulating tape).

Uses: To tie tape to form slings.

Comment: This is the only really suitable knot for tying tape ends together. It must be tightened and *loaded* to ensure the knot bites. Then the ends must be taped (bound) with insulating tape with at least 2″ (50mm) left in the free ends beyond the knot. *Even so, this knot will work loose and tapes tied with the knot must be checked every single time they are used.* In practice it is better to use tapes (either through nuts or free slings) that are factory stitch-joined prior to purchase.

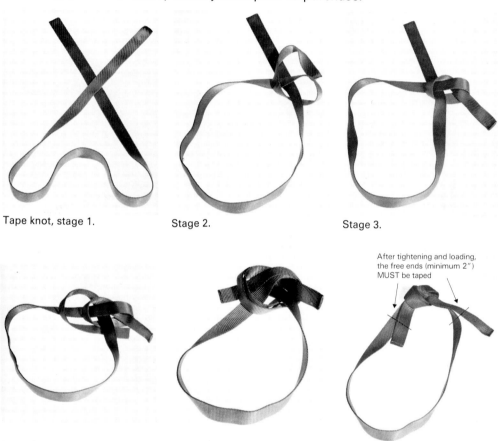

Tape knot, stage 1.   Stage 2.   Stage 3.

After tightening and loading,
the free ends (minimum 2″)
MUST be taped

Stage 4.   Stage 5.   Completed (untightened) tape knot.

PRUSIK KNOT

Uses: This knot provides a means of loading the main climbing rope through a sling at any point. When loaded, it locks a sling onto the main rope, but when released it slides easily. It is fundamentally used in Prusiking (a means of ascending or descending a free rope), but it also has an important use in transferring load to any point on the main rope: when taking dead weight off a belay in a rescue situation or in many other rescue and self-rescue techniques, notably crevasse rescues.

Comment: It is a very important knot to know. It is a simple knot to tie, being a sling merely looped through itself, and it is best effected with a rope sling of 5mm diameter. The larger the main rope, relatively, to the sling, the easier it is for the Prusik to bite. The photograph shows the prusik looped twice but if, in practice (e.g. a 5mm diameter sling on a new

9mm rope), the knot slips under load, then simply make another loop and it will hold fast. Slipping the knot after loading is equally simple if the thumb is used to pull back the outside wrapping loop. (See photograph on page 117 (top right).)

The Bachman Knot is the Prusik Knot wrapped through a crab, utilising the crab as a handle to slide the Prusik. However, in practice it tends to slip easily (the crab reduces the friction between the sling and the main rope) and does not offer a significant advantage over the basic Prusik. Therefore, I do not recommend it.

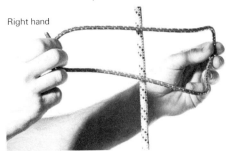

Right hand

Prusik knot, stage 1.

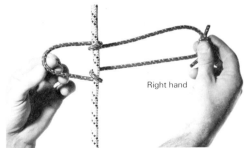

Right hand

Stage 2.

Stage 3.

Completed Prusik knot.

Note: if this knot slips with the illustrated number of loops, then simply add more loops.

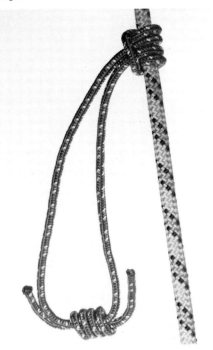

ROPE MANAGEMENT
COILING THE ROPE

The rope must be transported and kept tangle- and kink-free; correct coiling of the rope will facilitate this.

NEW ROPE

On purchase of a new rope you should take the trouble to uncoil it in such a manner as to avoid initial coiling kinks which may plague the rope for some considerable time. These can arise because most new ropes come straight off a large revolving drum and are not side-wound – the process employed by the climber. To avoid initial kinking a new rope should be first uncoiled as though from a revolving drum (rotate the coil around the hands).

ROPE MANAGEMENT THEREAFTER

Never throw a coiled rope onto the ground, hoping it will freely uncoil (unless it has been coiled by Alpine coiling, described later) for inevitably it will become badly tangled. If problems are encountered whilst uncoiling, it pays every single time to keep the rope in hand and to take time to weave patiently through the tangled coils, peeling them off one by one as they are freed.

As you coil rope, by any of the following methods, remove any kinks by twisting (twixt finger and thumb) the live rope so that the coils, in hand, lie straight and limp. If a rope begins to kink unduly, then it must be pulled through. It is best stretched fully out or even thrown back (retaining one end) over the cliff. In the latter instance the rope's own weight and the natural rotation of the free end, as the rope is taken in, will release the kinks. A rope that has been loaded, perhaps by a fall but especially by prusiking or abseiling, has an immediate tendency to kink and the above procedure of pulling the ropes through must be followed prior to coiling.

Once coiled, uncoiling the rope correctly is necessary to avoid kinking. Basically, the rope must be uncoiled in the same sequence as it was coiled. If you think about it there are four ways a hand-coiled rope can be uncoiled, but only one is the same (in reverse) as that by which the rope was actually coiled. This one is, therefore, the correct way to uncoil. Simply pay attention to the rope as it is uncoiled and if kinking begins to develop find the true uncoiling sequence.

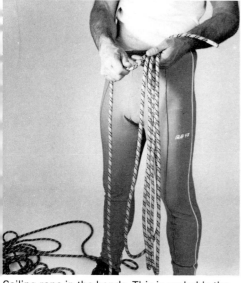

Coiling rope in the hands. This is probably the best method to prevent kinking.

Coiling rope over the head, stage 1.

Coiling the rope around the foot. This method was traditionally used by cragsmen when ropes were somewhat heavier and more difficult to manage than they are today.

Stage 2. This method appeals to the more extrovert and skilful rope coilers. It is not too good for wet weather conditions, since the rope tends to ooze water down the climber's neck!

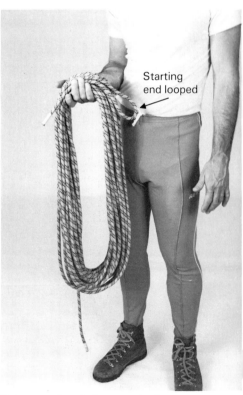

Starting end looped

Coiling rope around the knees. This technique wins the speed rope coiling championships!

Tying rope for all above methods of coiling, stage 1.

Finishing end wrapped around loop

Stage 2.

Finishing end fed through loop

Stage 3.

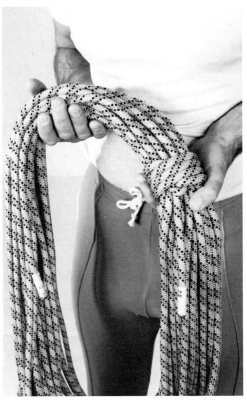

Finished coiling knot.

Carrying the rope.
This is the most versatile way to carry the rope.

Another method of carrying.

The Alpine method of coiling is fast to execute, doubles the rope and so halves the number of individual coils that have to be made, and has the distinct advantage that, once unknotted, the rope can be thrown to the ground and the live rope will pay out without tangling. Further to this, the incorporated carrying system, tied behind the back, gives maximum freedom of unhindered movement and yet the rope can be mobilised very quickly. The whole sequence is, however, fairly elaborate and its advantages tend to be superfluous to crag climbing.

The diagrams illustrate the doubled rope being coiled from the "free ends", but it is probably better to start from the middle (actual centre of rope) and to work towards the ends. This allows the last loop taken to be of the correct length and the choice of free rope (3 metres to tie around the back, less if going into the rucsac) to be made at the end. The slight advantage of starting near the free ends, as shown, is simply that they can be easier to find than the centre of the rope.

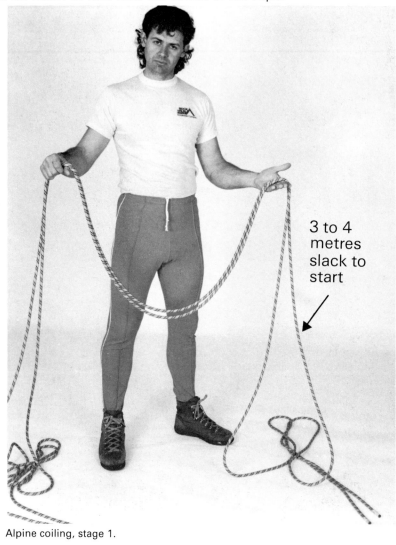

3 to 4 metres slack to start

Alpine coiling, stage 1.

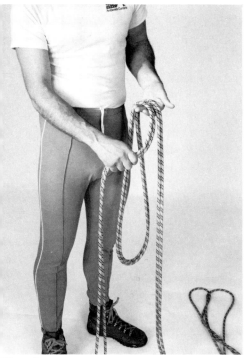

Stage 2.

Stage 3.

Stage 4.

Stage 5.

Stage 6.

Stage 7.

Stage 8.

Stage 9.

Stage 10.

Stage 11.

Stage 12.

Stage 13.

Stage 14.   Stage 15.

BELAYING

Belaying is the crux of all ropework and it has gone through many stages of development to reach the methods used today. When it was first decided that rope was a good way of protecting a climbing party, entire teams tied themselves together and climbed simultaneously, like elongated caterpillars, up mountains. It worked until steeper and more difficult ground began to be tackled, and then, when the weaker members of the team fell off, it was discovered that one falling climber pulled off the next. After a series of embarrassing disasters it was agreed that some other system should be found. Gradually, the rope between the climbers was safeguarded by one climber belaying the other. Later on it was discovered that things were safer still if the climber who was belaying actually secured himself! So, stage by stage, the modern methods of belaying were developed through hard and often bitter experience. There are, therefore, two vital components to be considered in belaying: the safeguarding of the climber by controlling the rope (belaying), which in turn can only be safely accomplished when the belayer is himself secured/tied (belayed) to the rock or ice.

BELAYING TO THE ROCK — ANCHORING

This can be done using solely the main rope or by clipping the main rope into a Crab which, in turn, is clipped to a nut, piton, bolt or sling. Generally, it is usual to use both at once and the golden general rules are:
(1) make the belay(s) as safe as possible;
(2) never take one belay when it is possible to get three;
(3) place the belay (or transfer your body position) so as to take immediately the load of a falling climber. The line from the anchor through the harness/belay to the "live" rope should be straight and should not have any slack.

Anchoring With Main Rope

If a suitable natural feature presents itself, then it is convenient to anchor oneself with the main climbing rope(s). This feature could be a tree or icicle or large rock thread, boulder or flake. There are various ways of anchoring but the following system is recommended.

Anchoring self – main rope belay, stage 1.

Stage 2. The main rope loop is passed, after threading around the natural anchor, through (behind) the harness belt (traditionally, this was the waist loop formed by tying directly onto the main rope).

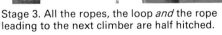
Stage 3. All the ropes, the loop *and* the rope leading to the next climber are half hitched.

Main rope belay – to be completed with more half hitches. The knot shown is only half hitched once, for clarity. In practice the knot and main rope belay are only safe when the knot is half hitched three times. The advantages of taking a main rope belay are its strength, assuming the anchor is substantial, and the fact that it can be easily adjusted for length, always allowing the belay to be taught. This latter quality of making the already loaded anchor belay tight, ensuring there is no slack which would allow the belayer to be jerked onto the anchor, is a very important consideration. The disadvantage of the system is that it does not easily allow the belayer to tie off a fallen climber (using a sling and prusik knot on the main rope) and then disengage himself from the system to go and seek assistance elsewhere in the event of an emergency.

Anchoring To Equipment

Traditionally, this used to be a sling, over a flake, threaded around a chockstone or around a tree, but in practice it can be any piece of equipment that can be secured to the rock-usually nuts, but it could be a peg or a bolt. In any event a Crab is used to clip in the main rope and the knot can be a figure of eight, an overhand or a clove hitch (if these knots are used, then it is easier to disengage from the belay system; first secure a fallen climber by means of a prusik loop from the main rope onto the belay equipment Crab). If it is desirable to adjust exactly the length of the belay, the above system of main rope belaying into the Crab is used. Alternatively, a sling can be clipped directly from the fixed equipment into the harness (a screwgate crab is recommended).

BELAYING THE CLIMBER — THE OVERALL SYSTEM

Looking at the main systems individually I will comment on the uses and relative merits of each. General comments on belaying will be made and heed should therefore be paid to all the different techniques described.

Using A Belay Plate
(Sticht or other plate, or figure of eight descender)

This system of friction breaking is the best and safest belay on rock or ice and it is the one that is to be recommended. Care when feeding the rope through the plate must be taken, especially if double ropes are used, but this method makes the holding of a falling climber a simple affair. In the event of a fall the rope is locked from passing through the plate: using one hand the belayer takes the trailing rope out to the side and so increases the angle of entry of the rope through the plate. The increased friction stops the movement of the rope. It is a simple and safe method.

Although it is easy to lock off the dead weight of a climber by this method, it is not easy to pull the rope in, through the friction brake, and so give the climber a direct pull for assistance (the latter action is known as giving the climber "tight"). If an erring second climber, following up a pitch, requires a pull to assist him, then it is necessary for the belayer to bend his legs, lock off the plate and then straighten his legs. The second man is then lifted by the belayer's leg power.

In the photograph on page 105 the lead climber is about to start off on a pitch (as shown in "Basic rope technique") and he is belayed by the second man through a sticht plate. Both the lead climber and the second are tied on to their harnesses with a figure of eight knot and the second man is clipped to an anchor (friend in a crack) by the same knot. Even though the second man remains on the ground he has anchored himself against the upward pull should the lead climber fall off onto his runners. Additionally, the second has positioned himself close to the rock and this is very important on two accounts:

(1) if the leader falls, he will not be pulled hard into the rock and possibly knocked out (any possible movement of the belayer should be prevented by the anchor);

(2) the ropes should be kept as acute (underneath) as possible to the runners because this prevents the runners being lifted out in the event of a fall.

The last two points may seem obvious, but time and time again I see thoughtless seconds standing away from the rock and (somewhat like Murphy and his barrel of bricks) if the leader falls, then, zip, out come his

Leader

2nd man

Screwgate crab

Belay plate

Belay anchor (for upward pull)

Sticht plate belay. Commencing the climb.

runners and, zap, goes the second, dragged headlong into the rock.

In the next diagram two ropes are being used and two anchors have been taken. The respective anchor crabs are tied with a figure of eight and a clove hitch knot. The important point here is that the direction of forces that will come onto the belay, should the second climber fall, all lie in a line, through the climbing harness, from the climber to the anchors. The belayer himself will not take any undue loading. In this case the belayer is sitting but the position of the belayer does not matter: he could be standing, as long as the line of forces acts through the harness to the anchors. To achieve this the belays must be tight, correctly adjusted (to spread the load equally to each anchor) and correctly positioned.

Plate belay. The leader brings up the second.

Whatever the belay situation, simply think of the end result if the belayed climber should fall. That final positioning you would reach should be the actual position in which you, the belayer, belay, i.e. with the load transmitted through the harness and not through the belayer.

Additionally, in the event of a fall it is vital that the supporting (loaded) rope does not run over a leg (especially vulnerable if the belayer is sitting) or any other tender part of the anatomy.

In the third photograph the belayer can take a pull from above or below. This is what every belay (anchor combination) should be capable of if the climbing team is alternating leads – which is quite often the case.

In this photograph the anchor consists of a sling around a tree into which the belayer is clipped with a figure of eight knot. Whatever type of anchor is taken, it must be capable of controlling the different directions of loading. If an anchor was taken on a nut, for example, then there should be nuts positioned for both an upward (because a leader fall onto runners results in an upward pull) as well as a downward pull.

Plate belay. Belayer is anchored for any directional pull.

Traditional waist belay. This is generally inadequate and is only used when speed is essential. The rope is passed around the waist and it is necessary to half wrap the "dead" side of the rope around the wrist. In extremes (I used to pull my pullover sleeves down to protect the bare flesh) it is more effective to half wrap both wrists with the rope.

107

Classic Belay Around The Waist

Anyone who has had their wrists and fingers burned or their torso almost cut in two and has experienced the dizzy feeling when rapidly being turned upside down will be no stranger to the sensations that can be imparted by the use of this belaying technique. It is a traditional method which is barely adequate to hold a falling second and it is inadequate to hold a falling leader. Its merits are that it is fast and simple to put into operation and can be useful if the belay plate is dropped or forgotten. An alternative with the rope over one shoulder and positioned diagonally across the back is vastly inferior and should not be used.

Italian Hitch – see *Knots*

Hanging Belays

On the harder, steeper routes, taking a belay without footholds is common. All the principles are the same as those outlined previously but it is also important when a second joins a leader on belay to transfer the loading to the anchors in such a sequence that no climber's system of tying on is fouled with the weight of another clipped in above it.

Using the Italian hitch.

Hanging belay – transferring the load. When the second man arrives, if he does not intend to lead through and before he is removed from the belay plate (taken off belay), it is important that he clips into the anchors in such a manner that he does not trap the ropes of the lead climber. Ideally, he should use separate crabs and should clip these into the anchors, under those of the currently belayed lead climber.

Alpine Coils

Taking Alpine coils is usual on easier terrain where the members of the climbing team move together. With ice axes it is possible in the event of a slip to arrest the fall (see "Ice axe belaying"). On mixed ground it is common practice for the forward climber to put on running belays and these are removed by the last man.

Alpine coils. Each climber takes coils over his shoulder. These coils and the rope leading to the next climber are secured by first half-hitching the coils and then finishing with either a bowline or a figure of eight clipped into a crab and into the harness (this is essential to prevent strangulation). The last climber takes further coils in his hand and pays these out or takes them in to regulate the amount of rope between him and the climber in front. This distance between the climbers depends on the relative speed of each climber.

ABSEILING

Abseiling (rappeling) is the planned and controlled means of descending a secured rope. It may be done on a fixed single rope or, as is more often the case, on a doubled rope threaded around a block/flake or tree or through the eye of a ring peg or crab so that it may be pulled down and retrieved from below. It can be done for fun, or perhaps to inspect a rock climb, but its most important function is as a means of safe retreat from a climb.

When I was a mere lad it used to be said that "Birkett abseiled faster than most can fall" and to the casual observer my mode of descent may have looked a trifle reckless. What they didn't know, perhaps, was that my father in his own quiet way had instilled into me the correct and safe techniques involved. Modern climbing ropes do not break frequently, yet there is no denying, statistically, that abseiling is one of the most dangerous functions in the climbing game. If you are aware of this and check every single component part prior to an abseil and then employ correct technique it is a safe and pleasurable activity.

Firstly, I will detail the different types of abseiling and will give individual comment and, secondly, I will conclude with a mental check list that must be strictly adhered to.

CLASSIC ABSEIL

This is the traditional abseiling method which was devised before the advent of modern equipment. Today it is to be used only in a dire emergency in the unlikely event of the climber losing all his other equipment, or for a single short easy angled abseil on a long trip where weight reduction is critical. As can be seen from the photograph, it is an extremely painful way to abseil and should not be attempted without a stout jacket and trousers to resist the abrasion and heat created by the rope sliding under the bottom and over the shoulders.

Classic abseil. (Note: the photograph illustrates the technique and rope position only – the clothing is totally unsuitable for this type of abseiling.)

Sling abseil, stage 1. Ensure the sling is long enough and that the crab is a screwgate or locking type.

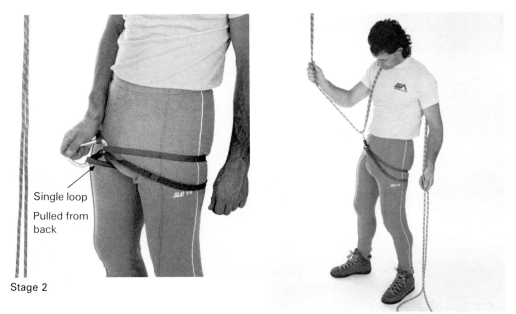

Single loop
Pulled from
back

Stage 2

Sling abseil. (Note: the photograph illustrates the technique only – the clothing top is totally unsuitable and abseiling thus would result in serious shoulder burn.)

SLING ABSEIL

This is another traditional method of abseiling which has been somewhat superseded by the advent of modern equipment. It has its place on rock up to vertical steepness but it should not be used for abseils in free space. It has serious hazards:

(a) it can badly burn the shoulder and/or neck unless they are protected with a thick (non-nylon) top;

(b) the rope can easily drag clothing into the crab and jam it or snag flapping clothing around the neck, resulting in strangulation of the abseiler;

(c) the climber must keep the low hand on the rope (not a natural reaction in a panic situation) at all times, otherwise a free fall would result. This severely handicaps the ability of freeing any trapped garments.

FIGURE OF EIGHT ABSEIL

This is the best and safest abseil system. Note the body position in the photograph on page 112; this position, with the legs horizontal and feet flat on the rock face, is the correct stance to be aimed at when undertaking any type of abseil. It is the feet that direct and control the body position when abseiling and it is essential to maximise control by keeping the body and hands away from the rock. The degree of grip exerted by the low hand controls the speed of descent (the low hand should always be kept on the rope unless locked off – see later). It is the co-ordination of hand grip and foot contact that enables a smooth and trouble-free descent to be accomplished.

Beware of clothing being drawn into the figure of eight by the live rope and ensure the crab is fast tight. Then just relax and walk down the rock.

In free space you will probably start to rotate; there is nothing you can do about this, so just relax and enjoy it. Don't be tempted to go too fast

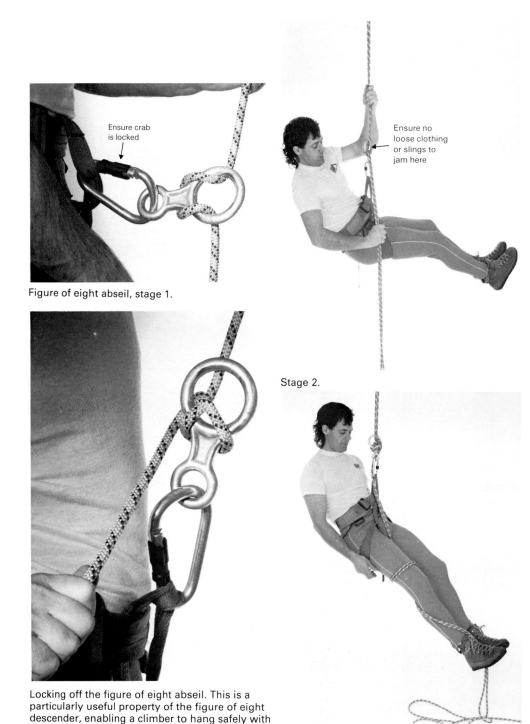

Ensure crab
is locked

Ensure no
loose clothing
or slings to
jam here

Figure of eight abseil, stage 1.

Stage 2.

Locking off the figure of eight abseil. This is a
particularly useful property of the figure of eight
descender, enabling a climber to hang safely with
both hands free.

Locked figure of eight with the rope wrapped round the leg. Always remember to wrap the
rope around the leg when locked off, just in case the rope slips when your hands are not
holding it.

until you know exactly, with the particular abseil device/method you are using, what effort and how long it takes to stop. Take care not to burn your hands; I personally do not recommend the use of gloves.

When abseiling over an overhang into free space it is usual to slow and control the descent further than just by using the degree of stopping power achieved with hand control. This is accomplished by wrapping the rope around a leg to increase the friction. This may also be valid on vertical rocks, depending on the thickness of rope(s) (and therefore the degree of friction) running through the figure of eight.

STICHT/BELAY PLATE ABSEIL

Although this is as safe as the figure of eight abseil it is an inferior method in a number of important respects. Sometimes the friction of doubled ropes through the plate hardly allows downward movement (in this case a crab clipped onto the rope between the plate and the harness crab, but not clipped into either, reduces the friction). In addition, the acute angle through which the rope is subject when passing through the plate strains and damages the outer sheath of the rope and if the abseil is taken too fast the outer sheath may well be melted to some degree. Also, the rope can be badly kinked by this method of abseil. If this method of abseil is undertaken it should be taken very slowly to minimise the above problems.

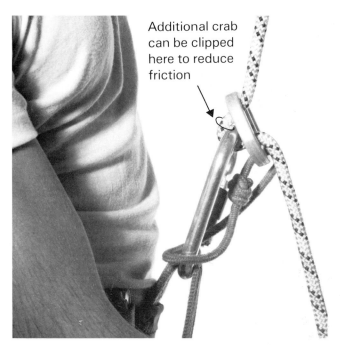

Additional crab can be clipped here to reduce friction

Sticht/belay plate abseil.

CRAB BRAKE ABSEIL — WIGGLY WOGGLY WAY

There are numerous crab brake systems but I think this is probably the best of them. It was devised by my friend, Rick Graham, which accounts for the ridiculous name. However, all crab brake systems are *potentially dangerous* and there are a number of things that can go disastrously

113

wrong. If neither figure of eight nor belay plate are available and you are forced to abseil over overhangs to reach safety, then this alternative may be considered. Ensure before use that you know for certain the configuration shown here, i.e. the crab gates are positioned on the opposite side to the live rope and the harness crab is securely fastened (screwed or locked). During the descent watch the configuration, carefully maintaining its relative structure with a hand above and below the brake.

Stage 2.

Crab brake abseil –
wiggly woggly way, stage 1.

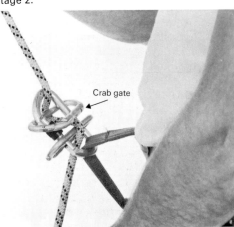

Stage 3.

GENERAL ABSEIL PROCEDURE

Before an abseil is taken by any of the above methods a suitable anchor point must be found. Make sure this is safe and can take the considerable loading it is going to receive. If possible use multi-anchor points in case of failure and if the rope is to be retrieved by doubling it around an anchor (then abseiling down the rope which is equally doubled) make sure the rope will pull easily around the anchor prior to the abseil. Treat any gear *in situ* with great caution and try to avoid abseiling with doubled ropes through a nylon sling. The nylon rope running on the nylon sling, when it is being pulled from below, will burn the sheath of the rope and will severely burn the sling (which may possibly fail if subsequently used by someone else). If there are any doubts about the rope running and there are going to be problems retrieving the rope (e.g. on a multi-abseil retreat), it is by far the best policy to leave a crab and some equipment behind – a sacrifice of a few pounds in exchange, possibly, for a life. Abseiling off threads around limestone is also another dangerous practice and should be avoided if at all possible.

It is good practice to "back up" an abseil anchor with others that are clipped into the abseil rope but are not taking the load. After the first person, the heaviest, has safely made the abseil descent, with the main anchor holding fast, it can be deemed that it will be safe for subsequent descents and the "back up" system can be removed.

Once a suitable anchor has been set up and the ropes have been lowered down, they must go all the way down tangle-free. You should ensure that the ends reach their required destination prior to your descent! If there is any doubt about this, then suitably knot the end of the rope to prevent the possibility of the ends passing through the abseil device and preventing you from abseiling off the ends of the ropes. (Yes, it does happen – frequently!)

A valuable safety precaution technique, in a forced abseil situation, where there is any doubt about the anchor (e.g. retreat from a large mountain face in a storm where time is important) is for the first person to descend the doubled ropes, to place runners, and to clip them to the same single rope, at strategic lengths throughout the descent. These can be subsequently removed by the last man to descend (others between first and last man making the descent should unclip and reclip these runners as they find them). This means that should the anchor fail then the runners will subsequently secure the doubled ropes – albeit with something of a fall.

If ropes are joined, note which side of the anchor the knot lies and which rope is to be pulled to avoid the knot passing around/through the anchor. The best knot, for running over ledges and rock surfaces and so avoiding jamming, is the figure of eight joining knot (see the knots section).

On and after the abseil avoid touching the abseil device, as this can get very hot indeed. Watch out for falling stones which may have inadvertently been loosened during the descent. At the end of the abseil it may be a struggle to release the screw on a screwgate crab. If this is the case, put your weight back onto the rope loading the crab and you will find it will unscrew in this position. (Not many people know this!)

Another safety precaution, in a multi-abseil situation, is for the first man down to tie the ends of the rope (figure of eight or overhand knots are suitable) into the next safe anchor point before the second man begins his descent.

If retrieving the rope proves problematical, then try altering the angle/ direction of pull to reduce the friction between rock and rope or alternate pulls on each rope, taking care not to jam the joining knot into the anchor. Sometimes, especially if done too quickly, the ropes will kink at the end of an abseil and to relieve this they should be "pulled through" as described in the section on coiling.

ABSEIL CHECK LIST
(1) Anchor safe?
(2) Rope around/through anchor and knot running freely?

(3) Rope(s) tangle-free and reaching ground?
(4) Harness done up and properly buckled ?
(5) Abseil system correctly fixed up?
(6) Screwgate crab screwed tight?
(7) All clothing suitable (if system used where rope contacts the body) and all clothing or dangling climbing gear, especially neck slings, well away from the live rope and abseil system (there must be no possibilty of trapping anything in the abseil device)?
(8) All OK? Yes? Then relax and go.

ASCENDING A FIXED ROPE

(Prusiking or "Jugging")

In an emergency this can be achieved by two line slings connected to the rope by the Prusik knot. If the ascent is pre-planned, there are numerous ascenders that are manufactured for the purpose. Whatever system is used, Prusiking or mechanical, the basic sequence is the same and is illustrated by the following photographs.

 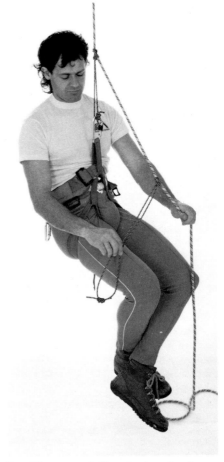

Prusiking, the slings in place. Note the longer length of the foot sling.

Prusiking, stage 1. Here the top sling is loaded directly from the harness and is clipped by a screwgate or locking crab.

Stage 2. The bent leg is placed in the foot loop. The loop is positioned as high as possible.

Top prusik knot loosened. This is done quite simply by using the thumb to pull back the outside loop.

Stage 3. Here the top loop is slid up the rope whilst the leg (with foot in sling) is straightened. The top hand grips the rope above the top prusik, for balance, and slides up the rope in advance of it.

Stage 4. The top loop is again loaded as in stage 1 and the process is repeated.

117

Jugging (prusiking using mechanical ascenders), repeating stage 2 of prusiking. Note that here two locking crabs are used on a tie-off/short sling from the harness to the top ascender. The foot sling has been knotted to facilitate the optimum movement of the leg from the bend to straightening. Many climbers connect this bottom ascender to the harness by means of a long sling as a safety precaution should the top ascender (or connecting system) fail in some way – although strictly speaking this is unnecessary.

GENERAL POINTS

Jugging is, of course, the superior method of ascending if one has the choice, but Prusiking is an extremely valuable technique in an emergency. Two Prusik slings should be carried (alternatively, the slings on nut runners or thin tape slings will work) if it is known that a fall will result in hanging in free space, e.g. when climbing above sea caves.

Ascending the ropes should only be done on a single rope which, ideally, should have a minimum diameter of 10.5 mm. It should also be appreciated that ascending produces a see-saw action in the rope and the sheath contracts and expands as the load alternates. Additionally any penduluming from side to side, which is usually inevitable to some extent, produces a sideways slashing between rope and rock. Because of this yo-yoing action the rope must be kept off acute edges or the sheath may literally be sawn through. If the rope is fixed from above, it is good practice to cushion the rope, with an old jacket or something similar, where it passes over the edge.

PROTECTING CLIMBS — ROPES AND RUNNERS

The advanced modern climber uses intricate protection systems involving both single and double ropes and the placement of many different types of runners, including combinations of gear which act as one individual runner. The lead climber protects himself, and importantly all other members of the party, on traverses by the placement of runners (more correctly termed running belays). The section on "Basic rope technique" and the photographs on pages 78 and 84 illustrate the fundamental principles. However, safe modern rock and ice climbing to the highest standards requires detailed understanding, and mastery of the craft, of both runner placement and ropework.

The general concept in protecting a climb is to obtain the maximum amount of safety from the minimum amount of gear placed. No climb can be made absolutely safe by gear placement alone; the safety of a climb depends on the climber's ability, knowledge and judgement. However correct use of equipment, with full knowledge and understanding of both its potential and limitations, is a vital factor in the overall equation.

A climb is, then, protected by runners, i.e. equipment is fixed to the rock or ice by mechanical action and is also clipped onto the rope by means of a crab. There are two main considerations here: the placing of pieces of equipment, consisting of individual placing (the nuts, slings, etc.) with the use of combined equipment and additional techniques, which have been dealt with in the chapter "Climbing equipment and its use", and the positioning of the rope/ropes in this equipment

A climber must be able to climb as naturally and freely as possible. To achieve this and to "runner" a climb adequately, a scientific system of rope management is necessary. Ropes should run freely without frictional drag, and should remain unhindered by cracks, edges, arêtes, corners or overhangs. To this end there are two systems of main rope technique: single rope technique and double rope technique.

SINGLE ROPE TECHNIQUE

This is practised on a rope with a diameter of not less than 10mm (although 11mm is the size most generally preferred) and is used for:
(1) straightforward rock climbs or mixed climbs which are simple to protect (see photographs on pages 78 and 84);
(2) straightforward ice climbs, usually vertical and without bulges or traverses;
(3) aid climbs or modern free climbs that are all bolt (or *in situ* gear) protected.

The advantages of single rope are its simplicity of use and its lightness.

The chief disadvantages are mainly that if the climb requires sophisticated runner protection for any deviations from a straight line, then considerable rope drag will be generated. On a multi-pitch route an abseil retreat will become more difficult, because a doubled single rope

119

will obviously only reach half the distance of double ropes. Additionally, on ice routes I always have the fear (irrational, perhaps) that a stray blow with the ice tool or a misplaced prod with the front points of the crampons may sever a single rope whereas with double ropes there would be a "second chance".

DOUBLE ROPE TECHNIQUE

This is practised on two ropes of distinctively different colour, which I personally would recommend not to be less than 9mm in diameter.

Double rope technique – separating the rope, stage 1. The leader has placed a runner (note the extension with a long sling) well over to the left to protect the bottom wall.

Runners on
right rope

Runners on
left rope

(Note extension)

Stage 2. It can be seen here that the leader has placed a number of runners horizontally opposite each other. They are "marginal" nut placements (with "tie-off" extension), only one of which would be unsafe, but there are no problems with drag when using double ropes correctly separated as shown.

Where it is vital to climb with as light a weight as possible, and it is thought the rope will not be subject to too great a loading, it is possible to reduce this minimum diameter, e.g. climbing with doubled ropes over relatively untechnical mixed ground or when soloing and carrying a rope in the sac to use in an emergency. Double ropes are used for *all* technical climbing.

The advantages of a double rope are many and most modern technical climbing demands its use. Correct technique allows sophisticated runner placements to be made whilst the ropes remain drag-free and run easily. Furthermore, they are especially useful for sea cliff or big wall climbing because they facilitate advanced rope manoeuvres (pendulums, tyrolean traverses and long abseils) and subsequent rope retrieval. Another major consideration is the fact that using two ropes gives you a further safety factor should one rope become damaged or is cut through whilst climbing – this is not an uncommon occurrence.

USING DOUBLE ROPES – THE MECHANICS

(These general remarks apply equally to Single Rope Technique.) The essence of using double ropes is to cut frictional drag and to this end one must separate the runner placements: one coloured rope goes to the left and one to the right. The position of the ropes as tied onto the leader's harness decides which rope goes where and thereafter these ropes should remain separated, one to the left and one to the right.

Under no circumstances, on the lead, should double ropes be crossed over, but just how the ropes are clipped into the runners depends on the nature and physical properties of the pitch. The following three examples illustrate different sequences of clipping the ropes.

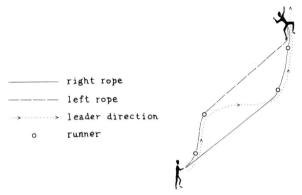

————— right rope

— — — left rope

·····> leader direction

o   runner

Double rope, clipping runners left, then right. Here the pitch goes straight up and then traverses to the right (e.g. under an overhang) before it again moves up. (There may be a number of such sequences, either to the right or left on any one pitch.) The left rope is clipped first of all, and then after the move to the right the right-hand rope is clipped. In this fashion frictional drag is minimised and the ropes run freely.

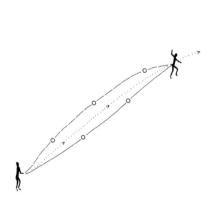

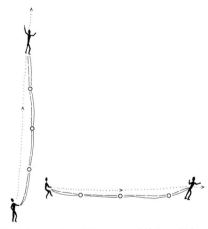

Double rope clipping, alternately left and right. If the line of the pitch is fairly regular, then it is usual practice to clip the ropes alternately.

Double clipping. This is used if the pitch is straightforwardly up (vertical) or across (horizontal), because of the gain in strength over a single 9mm rope.

RUNNER PLACING

The positioning of the ropes through the runners has been outlined above and the actual placing techniques discussed under "Equipment and its use", but there are some further points, both general and specific, which are extremely important.

DIRECTIONAL RUNNERS

On a hard and steep climb which utilises nut runner protection, particularly if for some good reason the belayer cannot get hard into the rock directly below a pitch, it is sound practice for a leader to place, as low as possible when setting off on the lead, a nut capable of taking an upward pull. This prevents the rest of his runners being lifted out in the event of a fall, due to an upward whip of the rope. A friend is the best nut for the job, because it can take an upward or downward load. If double ropes are being used and the nut placement is in close proximity to the belayer, it is usual to clip in both, whatever the method of clipping is adopted for the rest of the pitch. The nut is known as a directional runner because it directs/resists the pull and whipping force of the rope when a leader falls. (It also prevents a fall directly onto a belay.)

A directional runner should be used whenever the rope will act with a lifting action on the runners in the way illustrated in the diagram above. It happens in a number of different situations, particularly when one changes direction on a pitch. There are a number of circumstances when a tightened rope between the belayer and fallen leader will lift out all the leader's runners below the one that holds his weight. Rather than detail specific cases it is important that the fundamental mechanics are understood. However, the following diagrams illustrate a few instances.

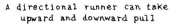

A directional runner can take upward and downward pull

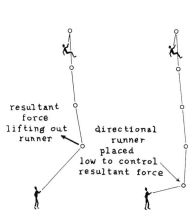

resultant force lifting out runner

directional runner placed low to control resultant force

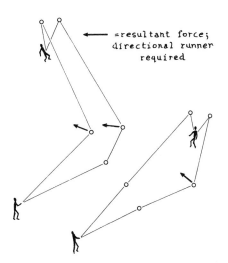

◀—— = resultant force; directional runner required

Leader should commence a pitch with a directional runner. The consequences of a leader fall, both with and without a directional runner, are illustrated here. Note that without the placement of a directional runner the first nut nearest the belayer is subjected to an upward force. If this is lifted out, then the same situation arises at the next runner. It is probable that all the runners will be "unzipped" in this fashion until the runner which holds the fallen leader is reached – if this should fail then someone is in big trouble.

Here are two instances when directional runners should be placed *en route*. A grasp of the principles is all that is required and then it is up to the leader to deal correctly with the particular set of circumstances occurring on his lead.

123

A directional runner can also run the ropes in a particular direction. For example, it may be desirable to keep the ropes away from a nasty-looking crack in which they would jam or, alternatively, to keep the ropes from running over a sharp edge or over detached boulders.

EXTENDING RUNNERS

The importance of extending runners to allow drag- free movement of the rope(s) cannot be overstated. Each nut, peg or other placed equipment should, as described in the chapter "Equipment and its use", be clipped to the rope by means of a "tie-off" sling. (Only in exceptional circumstances should a single or double crab system be used.) However, there are a number of instances when this alone is insufficent to prevent drag, i.e. when moving over roofs and through overhangs or rounding corners. In these circumstances *it is essential to extend the runners further*. This can be done using multi tie-offs (avoid clipping crab to crab) or, preferably, by using a long sling.

Extending runners to reduce drag.

PROTECTING THE SECOND

Care and thought by the leader must always be given to the second man. It is only ignorance and incompetence by a leader that puts a second in a position of danger through lack of rope protection. Also, it is folly in the extreme because any accident jeopardises the entire climbing team.

Traversing is the most serious occupation for a second. The commonest mistake for an inexperienced leader is to make the hard moves at the start of a traverse when he is safe next to the belay, and then to continue climbing with no runners because the climbing becomes easy. This leaves the second with hard moves to do and no protection.

124

Protecting the second on a traverse. Here it can be seen that the second on the rope has been protected correctly by the leader, both at the difficult start to the traverse and further along. (The crab on the sling is just visible.)

BELAYING NOTES

Use of double ropes does make belaying (with a belay plate) slightly more difficult; if a runner is placed above a leader's head, then the belayer may find it necessary to take in on one rope and to let out on another. Also, when the leader clips a runner with one rope he should suffer no drag or resistance when pulling up a single slack rope to do so. To assist the belayer the leader should shout down the colour of the rope he intends to clip: " Red" means the second should release sufficient red rope to allow the leader to clip the runner whilst maintaining the belay (he should not release any slack on the other rope). Only concentration and experience will make the above procedures into smooth operations.

LEADER FALLS

If a leader puts himself into a situation where he may fall, then he should have full knowledge that his protection system is adequate. This being the case, there are definite techniques involved in an actual fall. On a well protected technical test piece of the highest standard, on vertical or overhanging rock, it is usual for a leader to take repeated falls. Although these may appear spectacular they are quite safe, as long as he and the belayer adopt the correct technique. The belayer must take in and ensure there is the minimum of slack rope and the leader should jump/push himself out from the rock to adopt a parabolic arc when in flight. This method of falling avoids damaging contact with the rock as much as possible. A further tip is to keep the tongue firmly behind the teeth.

FURTHER ROPE TECHNIQUES

Further rope techniques become increasingly specialist and most can be worked out from the fundamental principles already outlined to suit individual demands. However, the following do warrant a mention.

THE TYROLEAN TRAVERSE

This rope technique is used to escape from sea stacks, pinnacles, etc. and to cross open space. It could be considered to be, in some respects, a horizontal abseil. Doubled ropes are used, with the ends situated on the retrieval side, so that they can be pulled and retrieved in the same way as after an abseil. The system is simply to clip the doubled ropes directly to the harness with a screwgate crab and to slide across, pulling hand over hand. Depending on the length of the tyrolean traverse and the tightness of the rope, it may be necessary to use an ascender to pull up past the half-way point (one is usually sufficient). The ropes sag under the climber's weight and the maximum depression occurs in the middle of the traverse.

Tyrolean traverse. The loaded rope shows straight lines to the climber on the traverse. Note the body position, with head and feet in line with the rope and arms outstretched. The climber is pulling hand over hand across the rope.

ROPE PENDULUMS

These are used to cross blank sections on big walls. A rope is fixed high and the climber pendules across on this. A number of swings may be required to gain sufficient momentum to reach the next crack system or feature.

ROPE SOLOS

There are a number of different systems that can be employed here and it is up to the individual to choose and modify the following two techniques to his/her own particular needs. Any system should be practised until the climber has flawlessly mastered the technique before it is applied in earnest. Whatever system is used, it must be pointed out that both techniques involve the climber covering the same piece of ground three times: once on the lead, then an abseil back down to recover the placed runners and belay, and then an ascent back up the fixed rope.

THROWAWAY LOOP SYSTEM

A secure anchor belay is fixed to one end of the rope and the climber to the other. Intermediate loops are made in the rope (e.g. every 10ft) using a suitable knot (overhand or figure of eight). These loops are all then clipped to a crab or crabs on the climber's harness and he proceeds to climb, placing runners and clipping the trailing rope as he goes. At the end of the free rope, when he reaches the knot clipped to his harness, he unclips the next loop and continues. The system has severe limitations, but Pete Livesey told me that he soloed (first ascents) both "Dry Grasp" and "Nagasaki Grooves" (at that time two of the hardest free rock climbs in Britain) using this system.

DIMINISHING LOOP SYSTEM

Here one end of the rope is attached to a belay and the other to the climber. The climber then attatches a mechanical ascender from his harness to the belayed end of the rope and as he climbs he slides it along by releasing it with his hand. He may do this in planned sections. If so, it is necessary to prevent the weight of rope in the body of the free loop pulling back through the ascender and this can be achieved by placing another ascender, again attached to the harness, in the opposite direction or by using a belay plate. Both hands must be used, one to hold open the ascender and the other to pull the rope through. Alternatively, it can be a continous process – if he can keep one hand free to do so. He places runners below the ascender and, in the event of a fall, the ascender will, theoretically, grip the rope and arrest the fall. Again, this system has serious limitations and I would not trust my life to it.

A more traditional and safer adoption of this system is to tie off a fixed length of rope and to clip it to the harness, ensuring when it has been run out that a new rope loop is knotted and fixed to the harness before the old one is discarded.

ROPE TECHNIQUES ON SNOW AND ICE

In addition to the rope techniques that have already been covered, there are certain methods of belaying, anchoring and rope retrieval that are specific to snow and ice climbing.

USING THE ICE AXE AS AN ANCHOR WHEN BELAYING

If ice screws, dead men or rock anchors cannot be taken (as illustrated in

"Equipment and its use") or if it is desirable to take a quick belay on relatively non-technical ground, then the ice axe can be used in a number of ways.

Ice Axe (Or Ice Tool) With Pick Driven In

As in the normal front pointing procedure, the picks are driven into hard snow or ice and a belay is taken, preferably through the wrist loop (to reduce the outward leverage on the pick). This is often used as a back-up belay to supplement ice screw(s). The best arrangment is for picks from both tools (ice axes) to be placed at an arm's distance apart so that the belay load is shared equally between the two.

Axe and Foot Belay

This is used only on non-technical ground where it is desirable to belay quickly.

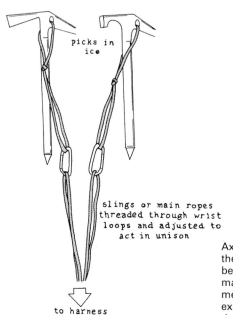

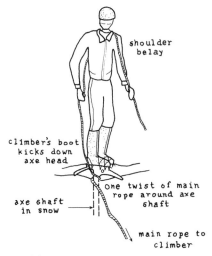

Axe and foot belay. The diagram shows the belayer standing with a shoulder belay. Such a position will take the maximum amount of load using this foot method. In the event of a fall the foot exerts pressure on the axe head, depressing it and the rope onto the surface of the snow and this action controls the rope. It must be stressed that this belay is only taken if speed is essential and in the practical situation, with ropes stiffened by the freezing conditions, it is usual for the belayer to kneel (still with one foot remaining on the axe head) and simply to pay the rope in or out with his hands either side of the axe – the shoulder belay is dispensed with.

Sharing load on placed axes. Depending on the quality of the ice and the pick placements therein, the load should be distributed evenly between the two. Note that the wrist loops must be full-weight tape capable of taking the load; otherwise, crab holes in the individual axes should be clipped.

Long Ice Axe Shaft In Snow

In some snow conditions this is better than nothing. The axe shaft is plunged vertically into the snow as far as possible and the climber belays to it with main rope or sling, getting as far below it as he can.

Burying Axe Shaft Horizontal In Snow

The shaft should be buried as deep as possible and the tie-off sling or main rope should be used (tied with a clove hitch) centrally on the shaft. In softer snow it is much better than the vertical method, but it really is only appropriate for emergency use and a Deadman anchor plate should always be used in preference.

OTHER (BELAY) ANCHORS

The natural strength of snow and ice can be used if an emergency situation arises in which the appropriately designed equipment (ice screws, deadmen, etc.) cannot be used. If the proper gear is available, then these alternative methods should be regarded as text-book niceties and should be left alone.

ICICLE BELAYS

Free-standing icicles (minimum diameter of 450mm/1ft 6in) can be used as anchors, but they must be treated with extreme respect. Curtains of ice in some circumstances can be holed (with the ice axe) and threaded to the same effect.

SNOW MUSHROOM

Size depends on the hardness and nature of the snow, but under the right conditions it can be used to belay to or to take an easy angled abseil from. Minimum size is roughly 1m (3ft) in diameter and 0.5m (1ft 6in) deep.

ICE BOLLARD

In tough ice a bollard provides a good anchor, suitable for belaying or an easy angled abseil, that can be cut in minutes, particularly with a tubular tool. It should be cut pear shaped and should be roughly 150mm (6″) deep and 450mm (1ft 6in) in length.

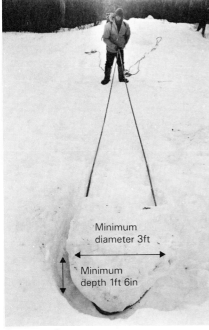

Snow mushroom.

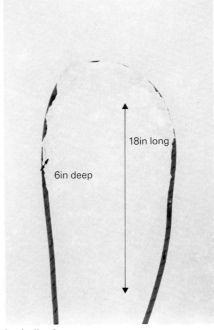

Ice bollard.

INTERNAL BOLLARDS

A piece of stiff wire 300mm (1 ft) long with a hook on one end is required. Two intersecting holes are cut with a long tubular ice screw and a thin tape is threaded through using the wire. The result provides a suitable secondary anchor.

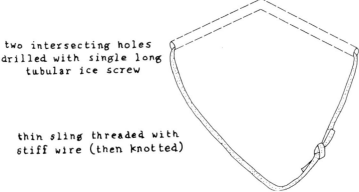

two intersecting holes
drilled with single long
tubular ice screw

thin sling threaded with
stiff wire (then knotted)

Internal ice bollard.

BURIED GLOVE

In an absolute emergency, with the right conditions, it is possible to fill items of clothing, e.g. woollen Dachstein Mitts, with snow (allow them to freeze and stiffen) and then to bury these sufficiently deep to act as an anchor. A rope or sling threaded around gives enough support, in ideal circumstances, to take an easy angled abseil. However it is not recommended!

ICE SCREW ANCHOR RETRIEVAL AFTER AN ABSEIL

Yes, it is possible, but it must be carefully practised and it is not recommended as standard procedure. A minimum length of 1 metre (3ft) of thin line (max. 5mm) is required and this is tied to the eye of a short tubular ice screw (screw in–screw out type). Firstly, the screw is screwed home, then taken out and cleaned. Secondly, it is screwed in again; this time the line is allowed to wrap around the shaft of the screw as it is placed. It should be free to rotate and the eye should be positioned above the screw (as shown in the photograph). The main abseil rope is placed (doubled) over the head of the screw and the line is fixed to the rope with a prusik knot. To retrieve the screw after the abseil has been made give one long continous pull on the rope to which the prusik is attached and this will rotate the screw out. (If it doesn't work, there will be problems!)

Ice screw retrieval, stage 1. The cord is tied to the eye of the screw, with the screw ready to be placed. As the screw is screwed in, the cord automatically winds around the shaft.

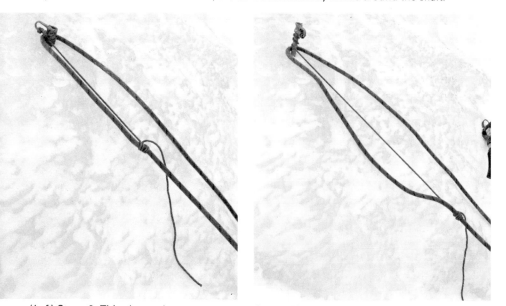

(*Left*) Stage 2. This shows the system set up: the cord is wound round the placed screw, which is fastened to the abseil with a prusik knot, and the abseil rope is in position. Carefully note that the eye of the screw, with the cord tied through it, is placed upwards, as shown. Because this technique only works with a short ice screw (125mm length) which is placed so that it is free to rotate, plus the fact that the rope rests only over the shaft of the screw (kept in place by the eye of the screw), it is only suitable for easy angled abseils.

(*Right*) Ice screw retrieval – pulling the rope. The rope should be pulled with one long continuous and smooth action. The cord, pulled by the rope, unwinds the ice screw and out it comes to fall down the ropes.

5
CLIMBING TECHNIQUES

"There's no substitute for ability" is a remark often cast in the direction of a struggling climber. This is not the kind of encouragement that a beginner or anyone finding the going hard needs to hear. However, take heed: whilst natural ability is certainly the climber's greatest asset, climbing performance at all levels can always be improved by both learning and applying correct technique.

Indeed, with the high climbing standards of today it is necessary for those who aspire to climb at the highest levels first to understand and then to practise climbing technique.

Climbing ability depends on the degree of knowledge of specific techniques and its application. The application depends on the climber's physical prowess (i.e. his qualities of strength, suppleness, balance, stamina) and his mental control.

This latter quality, that of mental control, is undoubtedly the single most important factor in climbing ability and achievement. I will cover physical prowess and mental control in chapter 7, and will deal in detail with techniques here. However, it is important to point out that an individual can have the best set of muscles in the world, he can be honed to perfection from hours of training on climbing walls and eating only the right food, etc., and he can know every individual technique to perfection, but if he does not have the mental control, to apply and co-ordinate techniques or to "stay cool", out there in front, then he will never be a complete climber.

CLIMBING TECHNIQUES ON ROCK

Most climbers use and co-ordinate many climbing techniques without conscious thought or preparation, just as a monkey swings through the trees. Even so, there are certain basic techniques that are fundamental to overall performance and they are not all obvious to everyone. For example, I was brought up on the rhyolite mountain crags of Lakeland and for a long time could not handjam; I used to layback all gritstone cracks!

In practice, a climb (even an individual move) involves a number of techniques and it is necessary to know each separate technique to master the whole manoeuvre. I will outline the essential basics which, when combined, will enable the climber to reach maximum performance. There are other specialised techniques and "tricks" (such as the "figure of four" which is often demonstrated on climbing walls where the climber cocks his leg over his arm and sits on it to make a higher reach than is otherwise possible), but these are not of suffecent use to justify their inclusion here.

I will begin where most climbers start: at the bottom. I will then work upwards to cover the complete picture.

FOOTWORK

Most of the climber's weight is usually taken through the legs on climbs – even on overhanging rock and horizontal roofs. Good footwork is, therefore, essential. The techniques do not require any illustration because of their simplicty (barefoot climbing with the use of individual toes has not yet caught on).

Modern boots allow the use of small flake footholds – the edge of the boot is placed on these; this is known as edging. On smooth walls and pebbles the front (toe) of the boot is "spread" over the hold. This is known as smearing. In cracks it is usual to jam the toe in and to twist, but any form of placement whereby the boot stays in place is acceptable. This is known as jamming. In order to make a high reach you should also practise standing, ballerina fashion, on the tips of your toes.

Another often used technique is foot changing on small holds. Here, to obtain better body position (maximising reach, power or balance) a climber deftly skips through onto a hold from one foot to the other. Note that both feet are off the rock together with this technique and it requires either good sighting or memory for the selected foot to gain the hold successfully. It should be recognised that memory plays a big part in accurate footwork. For example most rock climbs at Buoux take in pocketed overhanging limestone that requires precise and accurate memorising of the footholds, because once a climber passes them they are quite invisible from above.

HANDWORK

In the event of being faced with the choice of taking a handhold or falling to the ground the basic human sense of survival makes you grasp a hold. However the skilful climber must move beyond this basic instinct, and have the ability to use a wide variety of holds, whilst maximising his grip, pulling power, strength and stamina by applying the right technique. I will, therefore, concentrate on the more detailed aspects of how to make your hands hold and lift your body. On these types of hold it is usual for the rock climber to use chalk (see "Equipment and its use") and that is why the climber's hands in the photographs may look exceptionally white; it isn't snow – ice techniques come later!

Small Flake Fingerholds

Finger holds. The greater number of fingers you can get on one hold, the better the grip becomes. Try to get all the fingers on and maximise the pulling power by locking the thumb over the top.

133

Pinch Holds

Finger Pockets

Pinch grip. This is often used as an aid to balance. It requires high finger strength to use directly, but it becomes much better if used from the side as a side pull hold.

Finger pockets. Get as many fingers in as possible, but if there is only limited room (in this case a frog prevents any further fingers being inserted) remember that your middle finger is the strongest, followed by your index finger.

Handjams

A handjam is one of the best forms of a handhold. A correctly inserted handjam allows the climber to hang his/her full weight with the minimum amount of effort. In Britain it is the rough edged gritstone cracks, with their pebbles and sharp edged pieces of broken quartz, that offer the greatest intensity of handjamming. That's why the expert says, "You can always tell a gritstone jammer by his hands", to which the novice replies, "Because of the scars!" and the expert trumps with, "No – no scars!"

It is a very appropriate adage, for once the art of jamming has been mastered it causes no distress and is simple, safe and efficient to apply. Initially, the climber must carefully observe the crack he is jamming to find the best "placements", but as his skill improves, especially for marginal placements, he will begin to feel when the jam is best positioned.

There are three main types of handjam: the full handjam, the fingerjam and the fistjam.

Full handjam. This is one of the best and most secure handholds available. The hand is shaped, as illustrated, with the thumb pressed into the palm and the fingers and the back of the hand pressing in opposition.

Fingerjam. The best form is as illustrated, with the strongest fingers (index and middle) twisted into the crack. A variation for wider cracks is to cross the middle finger over the index finger and to jam these – it is not so secure, but it works! There is nothing like the thrill of bursting up an overhanging crack on fingerjams!

Fistjam. This is the most insecure of all the jams. Even so, it is a very good hold and is particularly suited to climbers with broad hands.

Palming is pushing off the rock with the palms. Reverse palming involves keeping the fingers pointing down, palms to the rock, and is the most useful handhold on a blank friction slab. Both are used in conjunction with other techniques.

ARMWORK

Straight arm hang. The climber "rests" with one arm straight (minimising the strain on the muscles) and "shakes out" the free hand, restoring blood supply and strength.

It is worth knowing that certain positions of the arm are particularly strong. A straight arm eases the strain to the muscles and this is the position to adopt as often as is practical. To "rest" (recover some arm strength) on steep ground, it is usual practice to hang from one straight arm and to shake the free hand to get the blood flowing in it and to rest it. Similarly, when the arm is bent, its strongest position is when it is fully bent, i.e. the wrist is pressed against the shoulder, and this is known as the lock–off position.

Locking off. The climber has locked off his right arm to enable him to reach for a high hold with his left arm.

COMBINATION TECHNIQUES

There are definite techniques that require a combination of both upper and lower body use. These should not be confused with combining separate techniques but are entities in their own right.

BRIDGING

This could perhaps be regarded as a pure bottom body technique but, in fact, palming is required with the hands to maintain balance.

Bridging. The legs are splayed, with the feet pushing in opposition. It is a very effective and common technique that requires a degree of suppleness.

SLAB/FRICTION CLIMBING

This involves a specific sequence of hand and foot movement, balance and momentum (speed), depending on the angle and friction of the rock.

Climbing slabs. Note the body position: the climber's bottom is out from the rock, putting the load through the smearing friction boots in such a way as to obtain maximum friction. The hands are low, one effectively pushing up and the other maintaining balance. Here the climber is using tiny flake holds and ruggosities, but if there were no handholds at all then the palms of the hands would be used. The high hand palming is for balance only and the bottom hand reverse palming (fingers down, palm flat on the rock) is to give frictional push.

LAYBACKING

Hands and feet are used in opposition. This fundamental technique occurs in a number of different forms requiring varying degrees of commitment.

Laybacking a corner crack.

137

Laybacking an edge, a wall move.

Laybacking an arête.

MANTLESHELFS

"Mantleing" is another vital technique requiring a specific set of movements and it should be practised thoroughly.

Mantleshelf, stage 1. Hands on ledge and a straightforward pull.

Stage 2. Up onto straight arms. Note carefully how the wrist is turned to face into the wall – this makes the move (by reducing the leverage) much easier.

Stage 3. The foot is placed onto the ledge and the climber's weight is transferred delicately onto this until he is able to stand on the ledge without use of any further handholds.

ROCKOVERS

This move occurs on a steep wall when there is a high foothold, and a low handhold but no other handhold within reach. The climber must then "rock up" to reach a higher handhold. It involves both dynamism, strength in the hand opposite the foothold being rocked on and a degree of balance. It is a very useful move for high standard wall climbing.

UNDERCUTTING

A low handhold is used in reverse, the climber pulling upwards on the hold whilst the force is counterbalanced with push from his legs. Again, it is a versatile and widely used technique and has a number of different applications.

CHIMNEYING

This technique is known by different names. It is at its simplest in a parallel crack where the climber can place his back on one side and his feet on the other. If the crack widens, it is usual to bridge across. It becomes most difficult as the crack widens past the comfortable back and foot position or starts to taper, narrower or wider, and it is then usually referred to as "off widthing".

LEG COUNTERBALANCE

This is another crucial technique in extreme standard climbing. The climber uses a high handhold on which his grip relies on correctly directed pressure. This, in turn, is controlled by correct body position. To prevent the body pivoting out of position (and hence the hand slipping from the hold) he counterbalances the body swing with the foot that is not placed on a hold.

A rockover. With his right foot high, the climber pushes hard with his left hand. As he rocks his weight over his right foot, the move becomes less strenuous (although more precarious) until he can reach a distant hold with his right hand. Note how he smears the blank rock with his left friction boot.

Undercutting. The climber is using undercuts on a steep wall.

Chimney/off widthing. The climber propels himself upwards by push and brace techniques. The main point to note in all the many combinations of push and hold that can be performed is to keep the hands low, as illustrated here.

Counterbalance. here the right hand pulls on the edge of the crack and is only held in place by the climber's body position as he gains height on his right foot hold. To maintain a leftward lean, and all-important body position, the climber counterbalances the tendency for the body to pivot outwards by placing his left foot (smearing only) out to the right.

141

ROOFS

The point to be made here is that even with all the many different types of climbing that may take you over a roof (undercutting, jamming, etc.) the feet play a significant role. Control with your stomach muscles the tendency to swing. Keep your arms as straight as possible to minimise the strain, move quickly and smoothly (to further conserve strength) and keep feet up horizontal by using push footholds, footjams and toe or heel hooks.

Crossing a roof. Keep the feet up, using available holds, and keep the arms as straight as possible to conserve strength.

MOVEMENT AND CO-ORDINATION

All these individual techniques and combinations are in themselves effectively useless! To serve the climber they have to be put together in a fluid sequence of co-ordinated movement. This will develop with experience and practice, not forgetting that the climber's "natural intuition" plays a large part in overall competence. If the desire to climb is there, with the will to apply and practise climbing and its component techniques, the individual will be able to climb safely to a very satisfying standard.

How the individual combines and co-ordinates his/her climbing is known as style. Style is the visual representation of ability. Some climbers appear to flow, unruffled, up whatever climb they tackle; others are more ungainly. Whichever style you have, you should always climb within yourself (in control of the situation) to obtain overall maximum performance on a route. Indeed, different styles should be adopted for different types of route. Most climbs are best climbed fluidly and statically where, traditionally, three points of contact are maintained with the rock. Yet there are moves, and even some routes which are steep and holdless, that require a dynamic approach. This means that both hands may be off the rock together as holds are slapped for or that just one hand remains in contact whilst the rest of the body moves to enable the free hand to secure a hold and in some cases a complete jump (no points of contact) is made. The important aspect of this type of climbing is both to maintain and to direct the momentum correctly. It is a form of climbing that requires a certain degree of energy and flamboyance. I particularly enjoy this dynamic style of climbing – which somewhat counters the popular belief that "dinosaurs don't dyno".

TACKLING A WHOLE ROUTE

Read the rock, the route and the prevailing weather conditions. With thought and experience preplanning helps maintain strength and stamina and increases safety. Thought, observation and awareness of rock type give the wise climber "pre-knowledge" of what may be required in the form of likely required techniques, resting points and runners. "Pre-awareness" to the climber is power, power to climb both harder and safer.

HAND CARE TECHNIQUES

It is said that high standard rock climbers never wash up because it makes their hands too soft! However, it is true that soft hands are a big problem to those wishing to climb for some period of time. Damage to the hands can ruin a climbing holiday.

It is a fact that skin does have the ability to harden, with time, to suit its environment and so the first strategy is to take it easy on the hands until this happens. When this fails and the skin starts to wear through, it is necessary to *tape* the hands.

TAPING THE HANDS

The tape used is clothbacked and sticky on one side. Typically, "zinc-oxide" tape is the most resilient and, of course, different widths suit different purposes. Narrow surgical tape is mainly used for the individual fingers or it can be used supportively for wrapping fingers together. In all instances where tape is to be used the hands should be clean (chalk free) for it to be successful. It is usual to treat the hands beneath with tincture of benzoin. (The tincture helps the tape to stick, hardens the skin and is mildly antiseptic.)

On long climbs with much handjamming in rough rock (typically Yosemite) some climbers tape their hands before the climb commences, thereby protecting the backs of their hands and/or fingers. (However, correct application of technique has largely seen a fall in the popularity of such taping.)

Frequent high standard rock climbing can produce a number of problems, with the hands suffering damage. Wearing of the skin occurs most often on the finger ends, which in its worst form can result in the finger end splitting under pressure. The technique here is to tape from the top of the finger downwards (in a wrapping action) and this gives the tape a better chance to remain in place when in use. If tendon or joint problems arise, it is usual for many climbers to tape the joint to give some support, or to tape a tendon-damaged finger to its neighbour, again to give it some support. (I am not advising this – it is just an observation; medical opinion may be that rest is the best cure.)

Skin-damaged hands must be kept clean to avoid infection and there are a number of hand creams available, based on fish protein, that quickly help the skin to restore itself. The only cure that I am aware of for tendon problems is rest.

CLIMBING TECHNIQUES ON SNOW AND ICE

One thing that the following text and photographs won't tell you, as you admire the shining axes and ingenious techniques, is that climbing snow and ice is very, very cold.

Remember it; it means that not only do you burn energy fast but also that your thought processes are slower than normal and your muscles lose strength. It is even more difficult to think rationally and effectively in the often harsh environment of snow and ice than when sitting reading a book in the comfort of your bivouac.

Climbing on snow and ice is by necessity a much more mechanical/ artificial procedure than climbing on rock. Apart from the clothing insulating you from the elements and keeping your vital digits snug, use of crampons, axes, etc. is an exacting science that requires correct technique.

For the climber there are two main groups of techniques: those required for climbing steep ground, and those for reaching and for leaving it, i.e. for making the approach and the descent. I will split the explanation of techniques into "Techniques On Moderately Steep Snow And Ice", i.e. on ground up to an inclination of 50 degrees and "Techniques On Steep Ice", i.e. on ground from 45 to 90 degrees.

Considering what has been said so far, and then what is to follow, there are three golden rules that should form the backbone of your ice climbing ideology. As the ice is cold, remember them well:
(1) practise the techniques until they become second nature;
(2) conserve strength;
(3) think about how each individual action will affect the whole climb/ climbing expedition.

TECHNIQUES ON MODERATELY STEEP SNOW AND ICE

If approaching a climb, it is best to have crampons on and axes quickly available before anything like steep ground is reached. Do not be tempted to reach the base of a mountain icefall, head-down on steepening ground, without at least an ice axe in hand ready to arrest a fall. Modern crampons, unless you are in soft snow, should be on your feet.

Footwork

Today step cutting can be regarded as a mere novelty; with short axes and crampons the old craft is redundant. If a step is cut, it is usually to rest in and to relieve the strain of front pointing. The adze of the axe is used where the snow is soft enough. One technique that may not be immediately obvious is to use the sharp edge of the adze first to cut either side of a proposed step and then to scoop out the centre with the adze full on.

Cramponwork/Flatfooting

Use of crampons at its most difficult on ice has undergone a complete metamorphosis to reach the current state of the art. It is now only necessary to know a few clear techniques and rules, and these I will give, as follows.

Cramponwork needs to be firm, positive and accurate: don't play, stamp those points in! On all moderately steep ground, when using the base of the foot (as opposed to the front points) and therefore *all* ten of the base points, whether ascending, descending or traversing, keep the front points of the crampons pointing *down the slope and the feet parallel to the slope.* I call this *flatfooting* and it requires a good deal of flexion in the ankle and must be thoroughly practised, preferably on ice, on ever steepening ground.

Whilst practising, it will become obvious that although it appears unnatural to ascend or traverse a moderately steep slope with the toes pointing downhill and the feet parallel to the slope, it is, in fact, the logical way to make all the crampon base points bite. First establish a comfortable rhythm and then experiment by changing the length of stride, hopping from one foot to the other and changing pace. Practice will also make it obvious when it is best to abandon flatfooting and to start front pointing.

Care is required with crampons to avoid impaling yourself, others or the rope. In soft damp snow, crampons may pick up the snow and ball up. Effectively, this lifts the crampons out of the snow, with each step you take, until the points no longer bite. The consequences are obvious and a systematic effort must be made to knock the side of the crampons/boot with the shaft/spike of the ice axe to dislodge the sticking snow.

Movement With The Axe

The axe, of course, should always be in hand on moderately steep ground. For ascent, descent and traversing it is used as follows.

Ascent in soft snow. Steps are kicked and the axe is used for support.

Flatfooting with axed for support. Note how the crampons are placed with the toes pointing downhill and the feet parallel to the ice. Adopting this position, the climber could safely descend or traverse the slope, and for short sections only (for long sections he would adopt the front pointing position) he could *ascend* the slope as shown in the next photograph.

145

Flatfooting ascent. Here the bottom leg is crossed over the top so a diagonal ascent can be made. It is only practical over short distances. In its pure form this should be regarded as a training technique rather than a standard means of ascent. Often front pointing is much easier and safer. However, in practice it is usual to combine both techniques: flatfooting and front pointing.

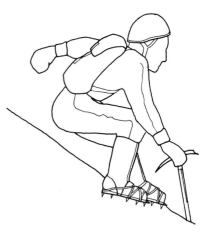

Descending. The body position is important here: the legs are kept bent and the ice axe is held thus (with the pick back), ready to adopt the arrest position in the event of a slip. It is also important to remember to maintain the flatfoot technique (toe pointing downhill, etc.), unless the snow is very soft in which case it is normal to dig in the heels.

Self Arrest – Ice Axe Braking

If a slip is made, it is possible even on quite hard snow to stop a slide by using the ice axe. With modern ice tools, sharply-angled pick and short shaft, it has become more difficult to effect this technique and quick reactions are required to arrest a slip as quickly as possible. Even so it works, but again it must be stressed that the technique is to be practised until it becomes second nature and until the climber knows its advantages and limitations.

This photograph shows how the axe is finally held in the correct self-arrest position.

The full braking position. This photograph shows the full braking position, with the axe pick dug in (in soft snow the adze can be used). Note carefully how the climber keeps his legs bent and the crampons up in the air (so they do not snag) and how he places his body weight onto the ice axe to control the slide. He pushes up from the stomach and this enables the weight on the axe to be varied as required. A common mistake with the inexperienced climber is to put the adze too near the head, which can result in a gashed face.

When moving over snow and ice the axe should always be carried, with the pick towards the slope, in anticipation of a slip. In the event of a fall a quick response is required to arrest the slide before momentum builds up. However, it is possible to find yourself in anything but the ideal braking position after a slip.

I found this out on my first winter trip up Ben Nevis after jumping over the cornice on Number 4 Gully (a safe descent gully) and sliding down in a sitting glissade. After reaching some considerable speed it began to dawn on me why my more experienced companions had strongly advised me to descend in the normal manner (walking down facing out) until lower down the gully. Basically, I couldn't stop and in my ensuing panic a crampon snagged and I began to somersault and role uncontrollably, very much like a rag doll. I arrived at the bottom (1,000ft below) with the wind knocked out of me. I was still holding my ice axe and I was still conscious; but I hadn't been able to stop myself because of sheer incompetence. Yes, I was very lucky; many more deserving individuals die every year on Ben Nevis.

The following systems enable you to stop and adopt the self-arrest position from various possible fall positions. They would have halted my fall and may stop yours.

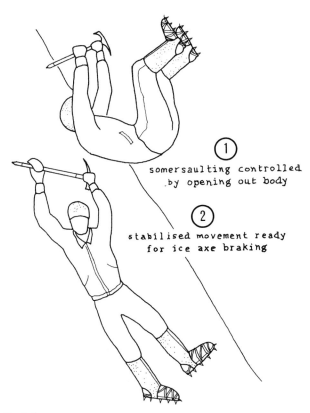

① somersaulting controlled by opening out body

② stabilised movement ready for ice axe braking

Controlling the fall.

Self-arrest – sliding head first on stomach.   Self-arrest – sliding head first on back.

A summary of the essential points is as follows:
(1) Carry your axe, with the pick towards the slope, in anticipation of a slip.
(2) If you slip, keep hold of the axe!
(3) Adopt a brake position as soon as possible.
(4) Arch your back, pushing from your stomach.
(5) Ensure your feet and crampon points are lifted well clear.
(6) Apply weight to the pick.

Glissading

This is a rather nice name for sliding down the snow. Under certain conditions it can be done standing up with the crampons off. It's fun and can be effected by leaning forwards to maintain balance, but it is more usual to sit. First, know that it is a potentially dangerous activity and you must be certain of the terrain below before setting off. Indeed, many

149

glissades have the habit of turning into self arrests. One common, often fatal, mistake is to misjudge the snow conditions. Remember that changes in temperature radically affect snow conditions. Soft snow during the day can be rock hard, and very slippy, for the descent in the evening and even though a glissade may be commenced on soft snow there may be hard ice below. Other serious dangers include rocks and ice protruding through the soft snow. Another good reason for avoiding glissading is that the slide usually results in snow penetrating the vital layers of protective clothing – this can be serious in a mountain situation.

Sitting glissade. The axe is held, as shown, as a lever over the climber's thigh, and the slide is regulated with the spike of the axe. Note that crampon points (better to remove crampons when glissading) have to be kept up as best as possible and there is a very real danger of them snagging – with possible disastrous consequences. If a traditional curved pick ice axe is used rather than the modern steeply dropped ice tool, then it is possible to use this in the snow rather than the axe point.

TECHNIQUES ON STEEP ICE

Principally, this means using the two front points of each crampon and the sharply declined picks of two ice tools, one in each hand. It is known as front pointing.

Front Pointing

Alternate placing of the axes and front points of the crampons enables progress up the steepest of ice.

There are two idealised sequences for front pointing up steep ice and the following diagrams illustrate this.

Front pointing.
There should always be at least three points of contact and it should be noted that the pulling power of the gloved hand is limited on the smooth axe shaft. Most of the load is transferred from climber to axe through the wrist loops: hence the importance of having the loops of exactly the correct length.

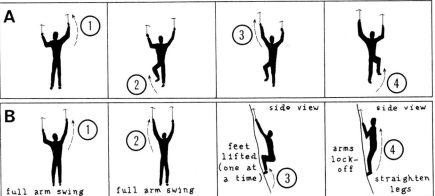

Sequences in front pointing. In (A), *alternate leg and arm method,* it is important, for full efficiency, to make sure that each axe placement goes in higher than the axe that is holding in the ice.

In (B), *arms then legs method,* the axes go in side by side with full arm swings (this straight arm position is the least strenuous in which to rest) and then, when the body is lifted, the arms bend to the lock-off position and the legs are straightened (again, a position of minimum strain on arms and legs).

Both these methods are idealised and in practice, because of varying ice conditions and many other factors, the actual front pointing sequence used is a combination of the two.

151

Placement Considerations

The sequence is actually dictated by the ice conditions because these determine to some extent just where the crampon and ice tool placements can be best made. In perfectly smooth vertical ice the ideal sequence will work and the correct placement of the crampons is with the boot horizontal, at right angles to the surface of the ice.

Placing the front points. Ideally, the boot is kicked in horizontally; climbers should be positive and should swing the boot firmly.

Sometimes the ice presents natural holds where more then just the two front points of the crampons can bite the ice; as this makes the climbing less strenuous they are frequently used. Additionally, and extremely importantly, when climbing thick vertical ice each axe placement must be made good. To achieve this brittle ice may have to be removed. Good positive swings should be made with the axe and it should be placed firmly. It should be understood that as one axe holds into the ice the free axe is swung in to make the next placement. It can be quickly seen that one bad placement leads to another bad placement (on an escalating scale), because a poor placement means that full strain cannot be taken whilst hanging on to it and therefore the next placement cannot be made using a full swing.

However, if the ice is thin then the climber cannot take full swings at it anyway, because it would simply shatter and leave nothing at all for the axe to grip. In this case the climber must hook the ice, using the pick delicately, over protruberances in it or perhaps reuse holes made by other climbers' picks.

152

Placement considerations. The actual sequence depends on the ice conditions. Here the climber is using more than just the two front points of his right crampon, because it is less strenuous to do so.

Falling Ice

Any large pieces of dislodged brittle ice that are about to fall (or are falling) and could endanger anyone below should be struck a deft blow with the axe to shatter them into small pieces.

153

Carrying Three Tools

On continuously steep water ice, where the air temperature is well below freezing, it is common practice to carry three tools (ice axes). This is done for two reasons:

(1) Low temperatures make steel brittle and it is not uncommon for picks to break en route.

(2) Carrying a short third tool, in a holster on the harness, assists ice screw placement. It enables two longer axes to be left in the ice, allowing the lead climber, if tired, to put his hands back in the wrist loops. Also, it is easier to rotate a screw with a shorter tool.

The above conditions are rarely encountered in Britain, but a third tool, a hammer situated in a holster on the chest, is sometimes used on mixed ground where it is preferable to climb with ice axes, each with an adze (as opposed to one with a hammer head).

Placing An Ice Screw On Steep Ice

It should be very carefully noted that a tubular screw-in type ice screw can be placed with one hand, the other arm remaining in the wrist loop, whilst a drive-in type screw usually requires two hands. Therefore, on unrelenting vertical (water) ice the screw-in is the type to use.

Placing tubular ice screw on steep ice. A shorter ice tool is being used here, which leaves two tools in the ice for resting. Note that the arm in the wrist loop is straight – position of minimum strain.

Resting alternate arms. The use of the third tool, now replaced in the climber's holster, allows the climber to alternate the loaded arm, so resting the free arm.

154

Look for a flat area of ice, with no protruberances that will either foul the eye of the screw or prevent full rotation of the ice tool, and place the screw virtually at right angles to the ice. A screw placed in a bulge (as opposed to a hollow) allows free rotation of the axe shaft, but ensures that the bulge is stable. Remove any brittle or unstable ice with the pick (this may also need to be done once screwing has started) and then chip a 2" (50 mm) hole. Insert the screw and screw in with your hand as far as possible. Then rotate it, using the pick or the spike of the axe as a lever, until the eye is firm to the ice.

Resting And Conservation Of Strength
The best resting position on steep ice is illustrated in the photograph on the right on page 154, i.e. with arms and legs straight. It is, however, still tiring and there must be a careful balance between the placement of screws for protection, which is even more strenuous than the actual climbing, and the continuation of the climbing movement, so minimising the time spent on steep ground. Hooking the arm through the wrist loop, locking the sling in the crook of the elbow bend, is another useful arm resting technique.

Exiting From Steep Ground
Pulling over the top of steep ice onto a ledge or onto snow needs care, because the straightforward front pointing mechanism is changed (it works differently horizontally). It is absolutely vital to keep the heels low as this keeps the front points of the crampons biting during the transition. Failure to do this, a very common mistake of the inexperienced, results in the front points shooting off the ice and places the climber in a potential fall situation.

Moving from vertical to horizontal. The climber uses his hands on the axe heads for support.

On ice it is usual to place the hands on the axe heads, thereby gaining the maximum body height before replacement. On snow the spikes may be driven in (shafts are therefore vertical), again with the hands on the heads to produce the same effect. If one continues in steepish snow to the top of the climb it is often easier to climb by alternately driving the spikes of the axes in, following the front pointing sequence but holding the heads of the axes or gripping the shaft beneath the head – using the axes like daggers.

Tunnelling Through Cornices
At the tops of most mountain snow climbs will be found a cornice. Normally these can be by-passed with a little prudence, but very occasionally they have to be tunnelled. Allow some time for this!

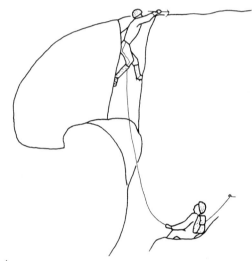

Tunnelling a cornice.

AID CLIMBING AND BIG WALL CLIMBING
To make progress using equipment rather than natural holds is known as aid climbing. Apart from short sections on Alpine climbs, aid climbing as such is now really defunct in Europe, but it is still practised on the big rock walls of Yosemite and elsewhere.

With the modern system of belaying using a belay plate, the ropework and holding the leader's weight on the plate is a simple matter and is covered fully in "Rope techniques". The gear, and its placement, is covered in "Equipment and its use" and directly following this, therefore, it only remains to make comment on the actual sequence of aid climbing.

The *etriers* are clipped into the placed gear and these, in effect, form a ladder for the leader to place the next piece of equipment/point of aid. The leader can clip his *cow's tail* into the top gear to take his weight or the belayer can hold him by locking his belay plate.

The usual system on big walls where much equipment (food and survival gear as well as the climbing equipment) is usually carried is for the leader to protect himself on a single rope and to trail a (thinner) rope up behind him. This spare rope is used to haul up the spare gear which has been placed in a suitably designed *haul sac*. The sac is usually hauled through a lightweight *pulley* to cut some of the considerable load to the climber and sometimes a mechanical system is rigged (*Yosemite Lift*: see "Safety").

As the leader hauls, the second *"jugs"* up the rope (i.e. mechanically ascends the rope: see "Rope techniques") the leader has fixed and strips out the fixed gear as he ascends. The process is repeated sometimes for weeks on end and the climbers spend their nights in *bat hammocks* or other specially designed portable ledges. Quite obviously big wall climbers are a special breed!

BASIC AID CLIMBING EQUIPMENT

The keyed in hard aid climber, depending on the rock type, uses a large variety of specialist gear. The following selection will be added to and modified depending just where and what the aid climber tackles.

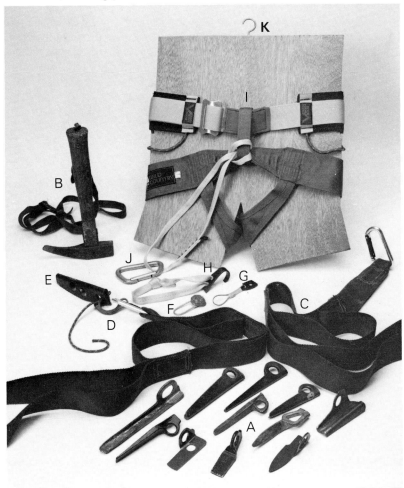

Aid climbing gear.
(A) Selection of rock pegs   (E) Bong   (I) Harness
(B) Peg hammer   (F) Bashee   (J) Cow's tail
(C) Etriers   (G) RURP   (K) Question mark!
(D) Fifi hook   (H) Sky hook

157

(B) illustrates a peg hammer. It must be sufficiently heavy to do the job and a small spike can be useful although is not strictly necessary. Beware of metal handles as they are not so good at absorbing the shock of the blows and this can prove uncomfortable and tiring on a long route.

(C) illustrates two etriers; clipped into the pegs these act as a ladder for the climber.

(D) illustrates a fifi hook; this makes it easier to hook and detatch an etrier to a point of aid. Note the attached cord: secured to the climber, this lifts off the etrier when the climber moves up. This saves energy and time because the climber does not have to reach back down.

(F) is a bashee, a lump of soft metal (lead or copper [known as a Copper Head]) cast on a wire loop. These are "smeared" into depressions and ruggosities with the peg hammer and the wire is clipped for direct aid.

(H) illustrates a sky hook. It is used as shown in the photograph below. It is most often used for direct aid or resting *but* because it can be easily retrieved by flicking the rope it can be utilised in rope manoeuvres including penduluming and abseiling (a look at the photo will show the obvious limitations). In *extreme* circumstances it can even be used as a runner placement in *free climbing*!

Sky hook placement. There are obvious limitations: will the rock hold, will the hook stay in place? They are actually much better than they look, but only experience will enable a climber to assess fully their capabilities.

(J) illustrates a Cow's Tail which attached thus to the climber's harness enables the climber to clip gear and rest without straining the arms or legs.

(K) is a question mark – is aid climbing ethical? (To all those bronzed gods, with bulging muscles, of the big walls, please, this is only a joke!)

ALPINE CLIMBING

It should be appreciated that the climbing of high mountains, Alpinism, often in remote areas requires sound application of many techniques. Firstly the very size and scale of the mountain environment should be fully appreciated. One must be both proficient and self sufficient, reading the conditions and understanding the objective dangers, to complete an Alpine climb of even the humblest technical difficulty.

Understanding the concepts of speed and timing, moving fast over non-technical ground and climbing smoothly, efficiently and safely on difficult ground are essential components. One must be able to balance the relative importance of lightness and speed (the lighter the load the quicker and easier it is climb) with that of having enough equipment and food (see Chapter 7) to complete successfully the climb and return to a safe base.

The Alpinist must have the mental and physical ability to survive in the mountain environment for extended periods of time. He/she must be physically fit, with stamina and strength enough to push on when it is important to do so, or to retreat in difficult circumstances. Mountaineers should be fully aware of the depleting effects of altitude and the extra demands this places on the body.

It is particularly important to assess carefully and plan an Alpine ascent, taking into account all the objective dangers (with due regard to both the prevailing and predicted weather conditions). One must optimise the available daylight on a climb. Generally this means approaching a route, covering non-technical ground in the early hours before sunrise, illuminated by head-torch. The climber should also be sufficiently wise and experienced, with ample provision in the way of food and survival gear (whilst still keeping carried weight as low as possible), to survive when all does not go according to plan (see Chapter 6).

Along with all the above qualities of self proficiency one must also appreciate that success and safety on high mountains is largely dependant on harmonious teamwork. Know and choose your partner wisely, remembering that a chain is only as strong as its weakest link. Extended periods of time shared in arduous conditions put a strain on even the best and closest of partnerships. Stupid things, such as the way your companion blows his/her nose, can become unbelievably irritating, and harmony depends on team members having a sense of tolerance, humour and honesty.

6

SAFETY

The English Alpinist, Edward Whymper, made the first ascent of, possibly, the most romantic peak of all time in 1865 when he crested that beautifully defiant angularity of rock and ice known as the Matterhorn. Yet it is his few words written after the disastrous accident which occurred on the descent, resulting in the death of four of his party, that are most remembered and quoted:

"Climb if you will, but remember that courage and strength are nought without prudence, and that a momentary negligence may destroy the happiness of a lifetime. Do nothing in haste; look well to each step; and from the beginning think what may be the end."

Knowing the dangers and being in the right place at the right time and doing the right thing has been the basis of the information covered in this book so far. However there are specific points of information that should be highlighted and certain procedures that every climber should be capable of mobilising should the necessity arise.

NAVIGATION

Basic map and compass work is simple and is something that all climbers must have the ability to do. The more complicated it gets, the less relevant it becomes to the practical climbing situation and it is only the essential basics that I intend to cover here. Anyone wishing to find out more on the subject will find numerous books, based on simple geometry and commonsense.

The point about simplicity and effectiveness was brought home to me in my earliest days of mountaineering. On arrival at the top of the great Scottish cliff of Creagh Meaghaidh we found ourselves in the teeth of a howling blizzard and rapidly encroaching darkness. I produced a map and my companion his compass – a small plastic device seated in the middle of a toy rubber tyre (Rick's "lucky bag" compass that had no doubt fallen from his Christmas cracker a few days earlier). There was nothing fancy here, just a basic tiny finger of metal pointing to Magnetic North. Setting the map from our known position at the top of the cliff and from the compass-indicated north, then reading the ground as we planned and executed our retreat ensured our self preservation. Using a slightly more sophisticated compass improves your chances of survival and enables more accurate bearings to be taken but the basic principle of orientating the map to the known line of magnetic north is the same and the important basics will be explained here.

However, at this stage, the climber should note that in certain localities, e.g. The Black Cuillin in Skye, magnetite in the rocks renders the compass useless by deflecting the needle away from magnetic north. It is therefore important for each individual to have a clear overall mental picture of his/

her position and surroundings at all stages. Do some research on the map and know the area and its dangers before you set off.

The latter piece of advice paid dividends for me when I was once below the cliffs of Stob Coire nan Lochan above Glencoe. We walked into thick cloud and snow, probably some 500ft below the actual cliffs, and the map and compass bearing taken to locate the cliff just did not ring true with what I knew to be the ground layout relative to our approach direction. So we sat down, hoping visibility would improve, to eat some sandwiches on a rock which we imagined to be under the cliff. A party traversed the the slope below us in their quest to locate the cliff. Fifteen minutes later the same party crossed above us and I hailed them to determine just what was their intent. They were convinced they had remained on the same compass bearing throughout their trek, i.e. they thought they were on the same straight line, which obviously they were not because they had passed us twice. The truth was that at our point on that boulder magnetite in the rocks was deflecting the compass needle by a full 180 degrees (completely reversing its direction). Originally, when they took a bearing with the compass affected by magnetite, they had walked out of the area until they had taken the next bearing which had given them a true reading, sending them back along their original course. Strange, but true!

THE COMPASS

The magnetic compass needle points north and the rotating housing, once north has been aligned with the needle, reads the degrees to the direction of the travel arrow. (Yes, those are all the basics you need really know – if you want anything else, read the instructions!)

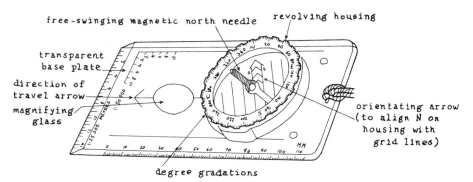

The compass. This shows a typical modern compass, with transparent, suitable for the climber.

SETTING THE MAP

With the compass and yourself at any known point, for example the summit cairn, it is easy to fix the true position of the map by just shifting it around to align the north grid lines of the map with the north point of the compass. Now you can compare the features on the map with those on the ground and can take a visual bearing to your intended destination.

This is known as roughly setting the map because of the magnetic variation which depends on your global locality (and the year) and must be corrected with the appropriate variation which will be given at the bottom of the map.

If, due to lack of visibility, you cannot actually see your destination, then you must fix bearings to it or to intermediate points of reference, i.e. another cairn, using the compass and map.

MAGNETIC VARIATION

This varies with the years and with your position, but all the relevant information will be given on the map. At present in, for example, Scotland the magnetic variation is about 8 degrees. This means that grid north is 8 degrees further east than actually indicated on the compass needle.

LIFTING A BEARING FROM THE MAP

This is done by setting the map and then rotating the travel arrow to the feature you wish to reach. The difference between the needle and that point is read in degrees and is known as the bearing. When the map is discarded and the climber follows along the bearing he must add 8 degrees (move the 'N' on the housing round to the east by a further 8 degrees) to allow for the magnetic variation.

Note: it is only possible to follow in a straight line to reach the referenced point. Once the climber deviates from that straight line the bearing is incorrect.

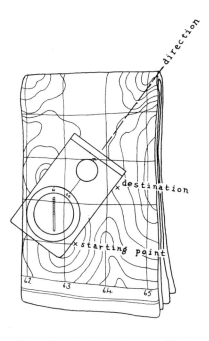

Lifting a bearing from the map. The bearing indicated is 20 degrees; add 8 degrees for variation and then follow, in a straight line, 28 degrees to reach the required destination.

Magnetic variation.

WALKING ROPE LENGTHS

From a known point in "white out" conditions it is imperative the climber walks in straight lines to keep on his correct bearing. To this end the technique is to keep roped up (belay in potentially dangerous situations) and for the second man to direct the leader along the bearing. At the point at which the second is losing sight of the leader, he stops him and proceeds to that point (then a known point on a straight line bearing) and the process is repeated until visibility improves sufficiently to enable a known feature to be sighted and the map set.

NATURAL HAZARDS

In addition to the topics covered in the first chapter ("Rock and ice"), there are some "classic" natural hazards that warrant individual attention.

STONEFALL

The danger of climbing a large face as the sun begins to soften the snow and ice, so releasing frozen rock debris, is obviously the possibility of stonefall. Just as lethal, but perhaps not so obvious, is the danger to be found on the humble rock climbing crag.

In Britain there are some notoriously dangerous crags where rock fall is frequent and difficult to escape. The danger does not arise from the natural loosening of the rock but from the careless action of climbers dislodging it. Always beware when climbers or walkers are above – even to the extent of shouting to make your presence, below, known. Some particularly bad areas which attract a lot of traffic at holiday times or weekends are:

(1) In the "amphitheatre" below Mother Carey's kitchen in Pembroke, Wales. The excellent climbs have loose rock at the top and, if dislodged, there is no protection for parties below. This area is a potential death trap at peak holiday periods, for there are many parties climbing.

(2) Below Clogwyn D'ur Arddu the narrow path is frequently bombarded with rocks dislodged both from loose scree and from loose holds. The area below the central descent route, below "Cloggy Corner", is the worst because there is much loose scree above.

(3) Pavey Ark in the Lake District, below the popular scramble of Jack's Rake, is another high risk area.

The rule is never purposefully dislodge a stone and always take great care not to do so accidentally. This rule applies even if you cannot see or hear anyone, for many people come and go without making their presence obvious. If you accidentally do dislodge a stone or pull a hold, always shout, "Below!". This is the universal British warning of stonefall.

CORNICES

These are wind-formed overhangs of snow and ice and, because they cannot be seen from above, the climber should know where to expect them. Basically, they are liable to occur on any edge between snow and air, i.e. on ridges, at the tops of cliffs and gullies. The danger from cornices comes when they collapse, which may be in a fresh or melting snow situation, under their own weight or when the climber walks too near the edge and either collapses the cornice or falls through it.

The climber must know where to expect cornices and should stay from under them in certain conditions. Climbers should keep back, well away, from the edge at all times.

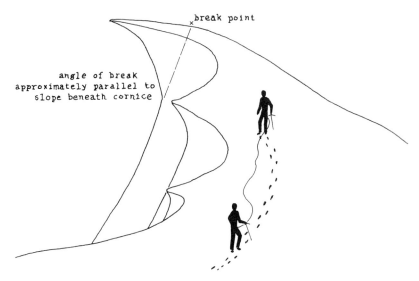

The cornice. These roped climbers (using Alpine coils) are traversing the ridge correctly, away from the point where the cornice would break away or where they would break through.

GLACIER TRAVEL — CREVASSES, SNOW BRIDGES AND SERACS

All glaciers have crevasses (deep splits and fissures). Some are obvious and visible, and some are hidden with a layer of thin snow over the top. For this reason it is standard practice for climbers to remain roped, usually taking Alpine Coils. In the event of a climber falling into a crevasse there is a standard procedure of *crevasse rescue* and this is covered later.

Crossing crevasses can be achieved in a number of ways, depending on their size and depth etc. Sometimes the climber chooses to cross by means of a Snow Bridge and the technique here is to test the thickness and stability by prodding it with the spike of the ice axe. If thin and delicate or if the snow is soft, it may be wise to crawl across on the belly to distribute the load evenly across the bridge. This may facilitate a crossing when a point load (the climber's boot) would collapse the bridge or punch through.

Hanging seracs of ice are always a worry and are potentially dangerous. The only sound advice is stay from underneath them, allowing plenty of room for debris slide, if at all possible.

The golden rule of glacier travel is: there are no rules! There are no rules because glaciers are *constantly and ceaselessly moving* and the stresses and strains are constantly changing. *Crevasses can open or close, snow bridges can collapse and ice seracs can fall at any time.*

Of course, there are certain guidelines which should be noted and followed whenever possible. Fresh snow is soft and, although it covers and hides crevasses, it is structurally useless, i.e. a climber can easily fall through it into the void beneath. So, stay off glaciers after recent snowfall (which you should do anyway to avoid avalanche danger).

Glaciers are most stable when most frozen, i.e. before the sun gets at them, at the start of the day, and after they have refrozen the sun's melt, as the night falls. Glacier travel is, arguably, best at night (depending on the capacity to see properly the terrain and features) or early morning. But remember, there are no absolute rules.

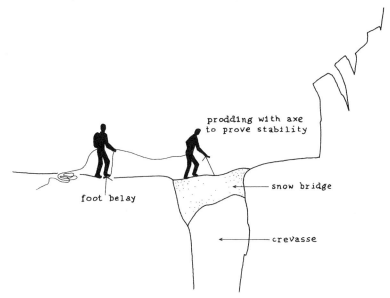

prodding with axe to prove stability

foot belay

snow bridge

crevasse

Glacier features. The climbers are roped (Alpine coils) and the lead climber is crossing a snow bridge, which he is testing for stability with the spike of his axe, over a crevasse. Some way above, ice seracs threaten. However, both climbers are wearing their glacier goggles and cream to protect them from the effects of the sun's UV rays, so even if the bridge breaks or the seracs fall they at least won't be burned!

Glacier travel in the sun has further serious hazards which, although not appearing as immediately spectacular as hanging seracs and open crevasses, can have a devastating effect on the climber and his chances of success. Both are caused by properties of the sun's ultra violet rays.

Snow Blindness is caused by reflection of the UV light from the snow and unless the eyes are protected with suitably dark (glacier) goggles the climber will suffer from it. Even though its effects are usually only temporary, it is serious, apart from the pain, because a blind climber is not a lot of use to himself or to others (this remark is not directed at blind climbers who purposefully plan to go on the hills and they and their team are suitably prepared). One extremely dangerous feature of this and other UV-related phenomena is the fact that the climber does not know that damage is being done until it is too late – so get those shades on right away.

Sunburn Protect those exposed delicate parts of the face skin with glacier cream – the nose, tips and tops of the ears and, most importantly for it is where the survival energy goes into the climber, the lips.

TRAVERSING A RIDGE

If a member of a roped two person party (alpine coils) traversing a ridge slips down one side, then the other jumps over the other to counter the fall.

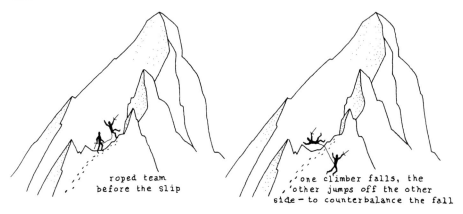

roped team
before the slip

one climber falls, the
other jumps off the other
side – to counterbalance the fall

Ridge safety! I wonder if anyone has actually done this?

AVALANCHE

The definition of an avalanche is: "dislocation of the snow over a distance greater than 50m".

The effects can be devastating and the best advice to the climber is keep away from avalanche danger. To do this it is necessary to recognise avalanche potential and to have some understanding of the basic forms.

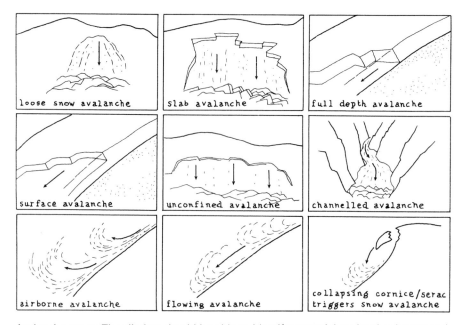

loose snow avalanche

slab avalanche

full depth avalanche

surface avalanche

unconfined avalanche

channelled avalanche

airborne avalanche

flowing avalanche

collapsing cornice/serac
triggers snow avalanche

Avalanche types. The climber should be able to identify potential avalanche danger and should stay away from it.

DETECTING AVALANCHE POTENTIAL

The two main points the climber should carefully note are that avalanches most commonly occur on slopes between 30 to 45 degrees and in freshly accumulated snow. However, it should be said that this is not exclusively the case. The lesser angle may seem surprisingly slight, but avalanches are common even here. On slopes steeper than the upper limit danger decreases because they tend to shed their loose snow before avalanche potential builds up. Snow that lays at a rate greater than 1" (25mm) per hour presents a big avalanche danger.

If a climber crossing or ascending a snow slope notices that the snow is breaking away in slabs where he makes his footstep, this is a sure (and alarming) sign of avalanche danger. If this happens, the climber is most probably in a position of grave danger and it is not easy to recommend a particular course of action. The climber should analyse his set of circumstances and decide on the safest course of action, and he should do it fast! Cutting through the hardened snow crust with feet or ski, hence cutting the stabilising strength of a snow slope, is a common instigator of slab avalanche.

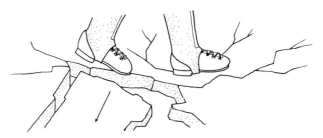

Breaking slabs: a sure sign of avalanche danger.

Weak layers in the snow strata are another major source of avalanche danger and the following diagram gives an indication of some features that create these plains of weakness in slope stability and that cause subsequent avalanche danger.

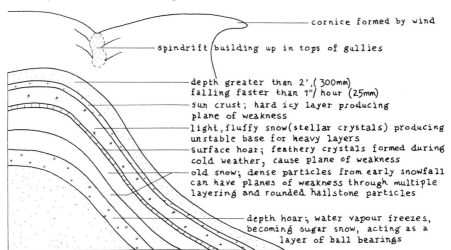

cornice formed by wind

spindrift building up in tops of gullies

depth greater than 2',(300mm) falling faster than 1"/ hour (25mm)

sun crust; hard icy layer producing plane of weakness

light, fluffy snow (stellar crystals) producing unstable base for heavy layers

surface hoar; feathery crystals formed during cold weather, cause plane of weakness

old snow; dense particles from early snowfall can have planes of weakness through multiple layering and rounded hailstone particles

depth hoar; water vapour freezes, becoming sugar snow, acting as a layer of ball bearings

Snow conditions producing avalanche danger. To determine avalanche potential one needs to know both prevailing and past weather conditions.

LOCALITY

Some localities are notorious for repeated avalanches and do so practically every season. These should be noted and avoided. Typical examples in Britain are the top of Central Gully on Great End in the Lake District and the basin below Coire Lochain in the Northern Corries of Cairngorm. Watch for this information in the guidebook.

AVALANCHE PIT

If you are unsure about a particular snowfield and you are well away from danger, it can be prudent to dig out (with axe adze) a pit as deep as possible to detect avalance potential. By prodding the exposed vertical face of the pit, either with the fingers or the axe spike, any erstwhile submerged soft layers – the plains of weakness that can cause slope failure and avalanche – can be detected. (See top diagram on page 167.)

Alternatively, if time is pressing, prodding vertically down into the snow with the axe spike may discover a weaker (softer) layer below the surface layer of snow. If this happens to you, beware!

IF AVALANCHED

Relax! Try to swim with the flow and as you feel the avalanche slow and settle make every effort to fight for the surface or make an air space. Anyone witnessing a victim of avalanche should, if unsuccessful in extracting the victim, mark the spot, if possible, where it was observed the victim was buried. Then help should be sought immediately.

CLIMBER FALLS — SELF-RESCUE TECHNIQUES

In exceptional circumstances where a fallen climber cannot be lowered to safety or cannot (because of injury or unconciousness) prusik back up the rope the belayer has two options if he cannot summon outside help. These are:
(a) to secure the fallen climber, disengage himself from the belays and leave (with some positive action in mind – one would hope!);
(b) to pull up the fallen climber.

SECURING THE FALLEN CLIMBER AND
DISENGAGING FROM THE BELAYS

I must stress that this is only done in exceptional circumstances. In Chapter 5, "Rope techniques", it was explained how to anchor to assist disengagement. This was simply to clip to anchor crabs using figure of eight, overhand or clove hitch knots or to clip the anchors with slings directly to the harness.

Disengagement is effected by taking the strain on the loaded rope through the anchor(s) and it is a simple principle which differs only in detail for each individual belay system. If a belay plate is being used the belayer frees his hands by wrapping the rope around his leg or foot. He then (this is the principle of the whole system) fixes a prusik sling to the rope and clips this to the anchor(s). The rope is released from the belay plate (or belay system) to be taken by the prusik sling fixed to the anchors. The belayer is now free to disengage himself.

PULLING UP THE FALLEN CLIMBER

The film heroes have no difficulty in pulling up a fallen climber on the rope. A straight hand-over-hand pull is all that would appear to be needed to effect the lift. In practice, whilst in some circumstances it is just

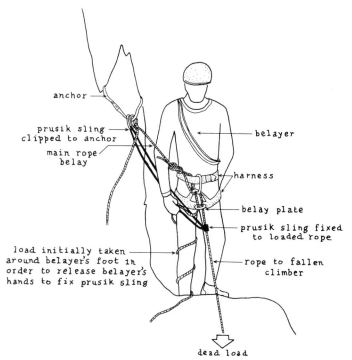

anchor

prusik sling
clipped to anchor

main rope
belay

belayer

harness

belay plate

prusik sling fixed
to loaded rope

load initially taken
around belayer's foot in
order to release belayer's
hands to fix prusik sling

rope to fallen
climber

dead load

Taking the weight of a fallen climber on a prusik sling.

possible, the climber will find there are two problems involved. The first is the actual power required to lift the weight and the second is holding that weight whilst the hands/body are/is repositioned for the next pull. However, there are a number of techniques that allow the climber both to lift and hold a heavy load. (This combined process is known as hauling.)

In the real climbing situation these techniques must be kept as simple as possible to be of any real use. There are two main principles involved in any practical system of hauling up a climber: (1) locking the load off through the anchors, and (2) easing the pull required to lift the load.

The most complicated concept of these two is, of course, the latter – that of reducing the pull necessary to lift. However, it is a concept that was used by ancient man, probably in the building of Stonehenge and the like, so really it is within the capabilities of most climbers to do without too much trouble. It is known today as the pulley system. In the climber's situation the crabs act as the pulleys and the details for each different system that I consider a reasonably practical proposition are as follows:

Belay Plate – Leg Power to Lift
If a fallen climber needs hauling a short distance, the belayer with belay plate can first squat with the load locked on the plate and then pull up the load by standing up – so using the leg muscles which are stronger than the arms to lift. As he squats back down, he takes the free rope in through the plate.

Straight Pull Through Crab – Utilising The Belayer's Own Body Weight To Assist: Yosemite Lift
Mechanically, this is the 1:1 pulley system (which means that the actual pull must be equal in force to the actual load to be lifted), but it is quite

clever because it utilises the belayer's own body weight to assist the lift and also provides a convenient system of locking off the load. The diagram is all that is required to explain the simple system.

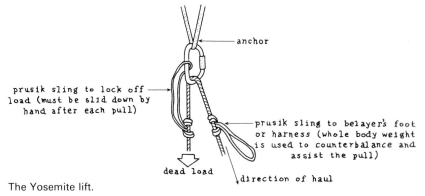

The Yosemite lift.

THE PULLEY SYSTEM
This system utilises the technique of the Yosemite lift but uses the pulley principle to reduce the required force to lift the weight. It requires (theoretically) only half the load's force to effect the haul and is known as the 2:1 pulley system. Again, its execution is simple and is explained by the following diagram.

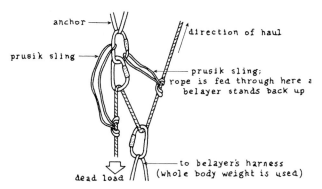

The 2:1 pulley system.

The above systems work when the action takes place in a vertical plane. i.e. on a rock face. However, the climber must know a system that can be used from the horizontal to the vertical in the event of *crevasse rescue*.

CREVASSE RESCUE
If a climber falls into a crevasse, which is quite a common occurrence when engaged in glacier travel, the chances are that the party are moving in a situation in which they have taken *alpine coils* (see "Rope techniques"). That means the second man must first arrest the fall by using *ice axe breaking* and must then take an anchor, with his mate dangling somewhere below him in a crevasse. The following system (theoretically there are many more) is a practical one in which first the belayer has (a) arrested the fall, and (b) secured the loaded rope to an anchor (usually an ice screw).

Generally, the falling climber will be in a position to assist his own rescue by partly climbing out of the crevasse, but if he his unable to do so due to injury he can still assist the belayer by using the following method which also utilises the 2:1 pulley system. If the victim is unable to function at all, the belayer must use the previously detailed techniques as best he can. The main problem here is the resistance against the running rope caused by the edge of the crevasse and the belayer should attempt to reduce this as much as possible – perhaps by placing a jacket or sac under the rope at the edge to ease the movement.

Once anchored, the belayer throws down a loop of spare rope (in the case when climbers have been using Alpine coils this is the rope carried around the climber's shoulders) with a crab in the loop. The victim clips this to his harness and then the belayer fixes it in similar fashion to the previously explained Yosemite Lift. This is best illustrated as below.

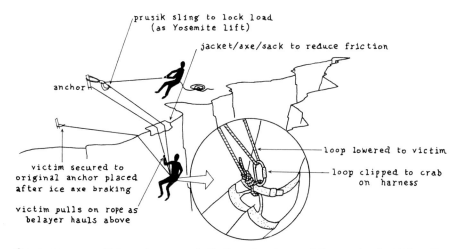

Crevasse rescue. This system uses both the advantages of the mechanical 2:1 pulley system and the arm-pulling power of the victim.

BIVOUACS

A bivouac can be planned or forced upon the climber. If planned, there are various options open to the climber both to choose the best site and to carry the right equipment. In any event, the climber must carry his equipment and he must balance its worth against the expense in terms of energy, loss of mobility and lightness. He must decide whether to carry a shovel, enough insulating equipment (karrimat for ground insulation (or equivalent) is essential), a down jacket (Duvet) and sleeping bag (Gortex covered is ideal) or purpose-made Gortex Bivvi bag, or to carry food and a stove. The forced survival bivouacer has only a basic climbing kit and must turn this to his best advantage.

The decision to take an emergency bivouac is a tricky one and, in most cases, I consider it is advisable to push on with the retreat. As a guideline in most cases, for example in the Lakeland Fells, one should always press on down to the valley, because civilisation is not all that far away. In the Cairngorms, though, the decision is a more complex one, the distances to civilisation are greater, and the correct survival decision may be to bivouac.

The most crucial action of any bivouac is to shelter from the wind. This achievement alone will probably enable you to survive. The second is protection from the other elements, snow or rain, and the third is to insulate the climber from the cold.

In extremes a scoop in the snow, with further protection from the wind by hiding behind the sac, is better than nothing. Once away from the wind it is quite surprising how much energy the climber can save. However, even if the bivouac is a forced one the climber is wise to make an early decision, before exhaustion or hypothermia develop, allowing himself time to locate a decent site and, in the case of a snow hole, to give himself time to dig it.

SNOW HOLE

The easiest place to dig is into the steep face of a snow drift or bank. One climber, using an ice axe adze, will take aproximately two hours to cut a snow hole big enough for himself. There really is no magic technique to digging a snow hole; it just means two hours of wet slog, of excavating and of removal of the the snow from the hole. Keep the entrance hole as low and as small as is practicable.

If two people are involved, it may be best for them both to work at the same time to keep out of the wind. Often the easiest way to facilitate this is to make two entrances, with the tunnellers aiming to meet mid-way (a body length) between the entrances. However, the disadvantage of this in an emergency situation is that both will not have sufficient room in which to huddle together, which is a vital method of retaining body warmth.

Whatever action is undertaken, the climber usually gets thoroughly wet, either from the snow or from sweat. With this in mind it may be best to remove clothing, storing it in the sac to keep it dry for when the digging is finished. Taking off most clothes and just leaving on the Gortex outer shell during the dig is common practice.

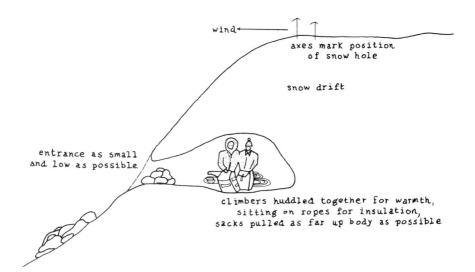

Emergency snow hole. Two climbers taking a forced bivouac, out of the wind, in a snow hole. Note the ground insulation – this is very important.

The important points in a planned snow hole are much the same as in the emergency situation, but the correct equipment makes it a much pleasanter experience. A karrimat supplies the vital ground (snow/body) insulation and a sleeping bag and duvet give the climber all the warmth required.

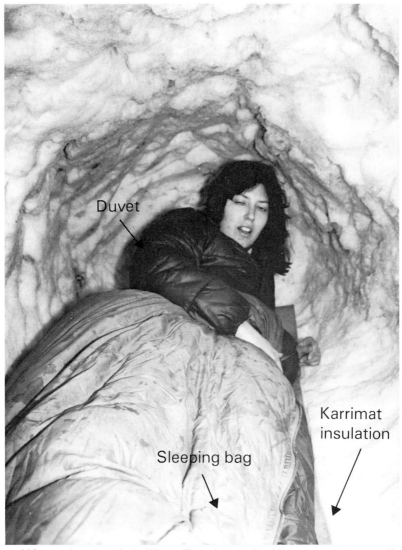

Duvet

Karrimat insulation

Sleeping bag

Planned bivouac in a snow hole. When effected correctly, this is a very luxurious affair.

The entrance should be kept as low as possible, especially if a stove is used. Stoves burn oxygen and generate carbon dioxide and, under certain circumstances, the highly poisonous carbon monoxide. Fortunately, the latter is heavier than air and will always sink to the lowest point – which should be the entrance. In any case, if cooking, allow a good circulation of air. If necessary, make a vertical shaft out of the snow hole (although this obviously reduces the insulating and warmth retention properties).

A snow hole can be illuminated by torch or by candle although the candle is the most practical proposition for a long term stay. A burning candle provides some degree of warmth and proves there is oxygen in the air, for a flame requires oxygen to live as do you! If the candle flame should weaken or extinguish, without apparent reason, then immediately get into fresh air and attend to the ventilation.

Condensation can be a problem which is exaggerated by boiling water or cooking. Again, ventilation is the answer and it may be advisable to fashion intended drip points in the roof of the hole if a long stay is anticipated. It is very important to keep the sleeping bag and duvet dry. In ultra-long stays, enforced by prolonged periods of bad weather which is a common situation in some locations, notably Patagonia, some climbers actually erect their tents inside snow holes!

ACCIDENTS

Never underestimate the seriousness of a situation or the dangers of shock or exhaustion. Above all else, remain calm and do not panic. Reassure the victim: be sympathetic and caring but be firm if necessary. Render first aid, as detailed below, but if a victim shows any sign of suffering spinal damage (i.e. pain in the back /inability to move legs) DO NOT move.

Keep the victim as warm as possible and protect him from the elements, if necessary constructing a temporary shelter – a rudimentary wall to act as a wind break. If there are more than one in the party who are hale and hearty, a fit member should be left to look after the injured man whilst the others seek help. If the victim must be left alone ensure his position is well marked before he is left. Leave something bright and large on the ground for detection from the air. If the victim to be left alone is confused, then it may be prudent to secure him to the spot.

FIRST AID

All climbers should attend a basic first aid course and the following notes are a rudimentary guide only. It is useful to carry a basic first aid kit, consisting essentially of plasters, lint and antiseptic cream.

In the case of an accident one should systematically check the victim for the following:
(1) breathing and airway,   (2) bleeding,
(3) broken bones.

(1) When breathing has stopped, if necessary clear the throat and pull the tongue forwards. If breathing is still not clear, turn the victim onto his side, with his head down and neck straight. Give mouth-to-mouth resuscitation if needed: open the mouth by pressing on the chin. Pinch the nose and blow into the victim's mouth. It takes a lot of effort and you must check to see wether the chest is rising as you blow. If there is no pulse use cardiac massage as well. Cardiac massage, although simple in practice, requires qualified tuition. I therefore recommend that this should be learned on a suitable first aid course.

(2) Even heavy bleeding can be stopped by applying pressure to the wound through a suitable pad. Press the pad, which could be a handkerchief or item of clothing if sterile lint is not available, firmly onto the wound for about 10 minutes.

(3) To detect broken bones determine where the pain is and observe any swelling or deformity. Immobilise the limb, as this reduces pain and prevents further damage.

If the problem is exhaustion/exposure or hypothermia, then stop and rest the victim, keeping him as warm and insulated as possible. In most cases a warm, sugary drink and quick energy foods are helpful. If necessary, with the above points in mind, go and get help.

RESCUE

For many climbers, who are rather noted for being a head strong lot, summoning rescue can be a hard decision. The lead climber must not only assess the prevailing conditions, danger from stonefall, expected length of storm, etc., but must also fully understand the state and capabilities of the rest of the party. He must understand the dangers, know the extent of a victim's injuries and inabilities and know that *a chain is only as strong as its weakest link*. A strong leader must make a decision based on these sound principles and he should not worry in the slightest about what other less informed individuals may say afterwards.

Many popular climbing areas are fortunate enough to have a good rescue service. Anyone wishing to seek help from these services must, in turn, help them as much as possible. If no member of a party wishing to be rescued can physically leave the scene, then they should use the International distress signal to summon help, as follows.

International SOS: Torch light – three short flashes, three long flashes, three short flashes, repeated after 1 minute interval. (Acknowledged by 3 flashes in quick succession, repeated after 1 minute interval.)

Whistle – follow the same pattern as for the torch light.

Mountain rescue services. Popular mountain areas in Britain are covered by excellent, voluntary, rescue services. Elsewhere, this service may be charged for.

Anyone who suspects that they may be rescued by helicopter (it is very common practice today) should endeavour to both occupy a site suitable for air rescue and to mark their position so it can be clearly spotted from the air. Beware of the rotor blades and be prepared for the considerable downdraught which can blow unsecured equipment away and viciously lower the air temperature.

If possible (preferably) two strong, fit members of the party should be sent to summon rescue. Before they are dispatched they should be clearly aware of the the position and state of those who are to be rescued. When they make contact with the rescue services (in Britain dial 999 at any telephone – no money is required) they should keep calm and give the required details clearly and accurately. At this stage it is possible to save a lot of time and effort by just being calm, clear and accurate. Party members should take a little time if necessary; if confused, they should just start from the beginning and tell the whole story – the time of telling is nothing compared with the time that will be saved in giving accurate and factual information.

CARRYING OF VICTIMS

If, for example, in a wilderness area, it is desirable for the party to carry the victim out, then there are a number of improvised systems that are of use, from the straightforward piggy-back to the rope stretcher. Depending on the available materials and the injuries of the victim, most methods are best left to the ingenuity of the climber. However, the rope stretcher (requiring only one single rope and nothing else) which needs a minimum of two to carry it (preferably more) is worth knowing how to construct. It is simple to do, but needs practice to get perfect. It can be made in 15 minutes by a competent, well rehearsed constructor.

Single rope stretcher. A single climbing rope and practice are all that are required to construct a rope stretcher. A minimum of two men is needed to carry the victim, but more carriers are preferable.

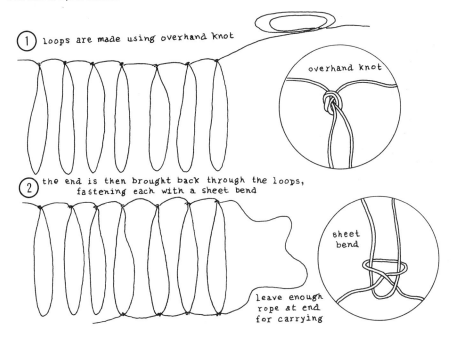

① loops are made using overhand knot

overhand knot

② the end is then brought back through the loops, fastening each with a sheet bend

sheet bend

leave enough rope at end for carrying

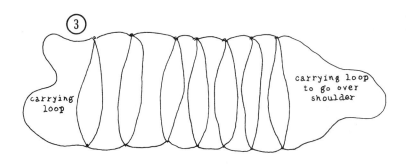

③

carrying loop

carrying loop to go over shoulder

7

PERFORMANCE

The units that have built the climbing picture so far are the essential items of knowledge that every competent climber should know and which should become second nature. Knowledge alone, however, is not enough. Climbing performance and achievement depend on a number of very important factors which have not yet been fully discussed. Each individual climber's concept of achievement, and therefore the performance required to gain that achievement, is strikingly different and it is no simple process to separate and categorise performance and achievement. Yet to present a meaningful message I think it is necessary to do this; it will also help the critic searching for easily identified unconventionality in the process of earning his "few dollars". Therefore I shall tackle the question of performance under the following divisions: philosophy, training, diet and ethics.

Firstly, I must look more closely at the concept of achievement. Climbing will never be like a conventional game, played with fixed rules merely to win or to beat an opponent. Certainly, there is the challenge to set an objective and achieve it, to push hard and express the naturally competitive side of human nature. But, thankfully, climbing offers much more than this for those who wish to look a little further.

It was the French mountain guide and Alpinist, Lionel Terray, who said as much in just the few words that titled his autobiography, "Conquistadors of the Useless". For the young, ambitious climber it may seem paradoxical that one who climbed with such brilliance and who achieved so much should name the title of a book in such a manner. I, for one, found this to be the case.

Some time later, with certain ambitions achieved, I discussed with a friend my disillusionment with the climbing world as I saw it. As we parted, he placed a newspaper on which he had been doodling on the table. The open page had a photograph of some sportsmen with glittering trophies in their hands and from a bubble out of the mouth of one was written in ink, "Conquistadors of the Useless"!

I laughed at those ridiculous prizes and in doing so laughed at myself. Outside my door lay the world of rock and ice and an appreciation of this, as the young climber will learn, is worth more than ambition fulfilled or unfulfilled. Climbing is many different things to many different people and climbers are very special people; it is no simple game, with trinkets given for considered performance – it is a way of life that is open to all those who wish to follow it.

PHILOSOPHY

There is no doubt that the climber's weakest "muscle" is most often the mind. Climbing ability can be seen to come from two main components: knowledge of technique and the application of that technique. In turn, the application involves two fundamental qualities: mental control and physical prowess. Whilst one is, of course, useless without the other, I would suggest that, depending on the nature and standard of climb you wish to undertake, it is mental control that is the most important and influential aspect in climbing performance.

Let's look at the nervous and reluctant beginner taking his first steps. He places his boot on a hold and tries all ways to make that foot slip off. He is expecting to say, "Look, I just can't do it, it's impossible". Eventually he will stand up and, much to his extreme amazement, his boot will stay put. As he progresses he gains confidence, starts to think, " I can do it", and actually begins to enjoy the climb! The negative mental attitude, self-doubt and fear, begins to turn into a positive approach. It is this positive, confident approach, the feeling that "I can do it", that gives the climber the power to achieve top performance. Of course, some degree of fear and excitement always remains even in the coolest climber; the surge of adrenalin generated before the big push or commitment is important to success and to providing challenge and enjoyment.

So, how do you acquire confidence? Well, some people are over-confident. They have ambitions and belief in themselves way beyond their ability to climb. Often their climbing career comes to a premature end, or if they are lucky and survive the fall they learn to temper confidence with ability. This is the answer for all; build up the difficulty of the climb and if you find you're not enjoying climbs because they are too difficult then move down a grade. Over a succession of climbs, confidence will grow as you realise just what you can do.

Gradually improving the grade, and enjoying your climbing, is the best way to gain confidence and climb harder. Combine this with dedication and training and you will reach maximum climbing performance.

It is necessary to approach every climb with confidence and the correct positive mental attitude. Different people do this in different ways, but the quiet period of "psyching up" is extremely important to perfor-mance. Psyching up can be thought of as a period of both self and route assessment – a period of mental questioning and answering before a climb. For many it runs as follows: "I am fit; I am strong; I know the ropework and protection required on this route and I can do it; I know the rock/ice type and as much about the climb as possible; I understand both the physical and psychological nature of this climb; I'm going to try my best."

Of course, only you will ever know what is going on in your own mind and the thought processes to be positive must match up with the true facts – you can't fool yourself with a few hundred feet of vertical and overhanging ground towering overhead: the buck begins and ends with you. So, you must really be prepared and have good equipment manage-ment, be in good shape, have information about the climb, match the climb to your personal ability, have an overall plan of action for the climbing day and, if necessary, know when to retreat.

At this point the mental energy required is probably at a peak, for once you start climbing you are "switched on" and much of what you do comes naturally. At this point many decide they cannot meet the demands made but, when faced with the actual reality, make up some excuse or other. This was best summed up by Tom Patey in his amusing article, "The Art Of Climbing Down Gracefully" when he described excuses for, some imaginary and some real, not actually climbing. These included: the "off-form" ploy, the "too much like hard work" ploy, the "chossy climb" ploy, the "ice man" ploy (for those about to tackle a rock climb), the "wrong gear ploy", the "responsible family man" ploy, etc. All were excuses for someone not actually wanting to tackle a climb, whereas all the would-be climber was actually saying was simply, "No, I've done my self-assessment. I've looked at how I feel and at the challenge to be met, and I'm just not up to it."

It's true to say that even the very best climbers find this to be the case in some place or at one time or another. The great Lakeland rock climber, Arthur Dolphin, once retreated from a comparatively simple climb in Wales and under questioning from the pack he simply, and honestly, replied: "I wasn't good enough – on the day".

Coolness, calmness and confidence are essential before and on the climb. Sometimes a particular situation will arise on a climb which threatens to frighten the climber and destroy his confidence. My father, Jim Birkett, instilled in me the fact that it does no good at all to panic and one should just relax and keep cool – if you are going to fall, so be it: there is nothing you can do about it, so you might as well keep calm! (He never fell in his entire climbing career – in those days you could not afford to, because protection for the leader was virtually non-existent.) If the climb is too difficult or too dangerous for the day, then know when to retreat. A good climber knows his limitations and returns to climb on another day.

OUTLOOK

A climber should never feel inhibited by the preferences of others: climbing is infinitely diverse and will always mean different things to different people. There is so much to be found in this world of rock and ice that one should not imagine for a moment that any particular individual's branch or speciality is the ultimate achievement.

For those in skin-hugging multi-coloured tights, splashing the rock with white chalk and athletic brilliance as they proceed from protection bolt to protection bolt, physical performance may be everything – this is fine. To the ice climber on eggshell thin ice 100 ft out from his last runner, a thread around an icicle, stretching his neck is the greatest thrill – so be it: he chose it. A chap who lights his pipe whilst reclining on a heather ledge midway up a climb, chats with his companions and observes, far below, a shaft of sunlight suddenly lighting the black lochan silver, experiences the wonder of the natural world. Each of these observations is a magnificent part of the climbing privilege.

For me, climbing interest and enjoyment could, perhaps, be categorised into three main divisions: the difficult climbing challenge, appreciation of the natural environment and joy of companionship. Sometimes one is more important than the other, but they are never mutually exclusive.

EGO

The very nature of climbing, the required self-confidence and power to make the difficult climb, can in certain circumstances and in varying degrees result in an inflation of the ego. Every climber, to some extent, loves to feel superior by virtue of performance. It's just part of the game and part of human nature. Thankfully, it is usual to find, however, that the more skilfully gifted and accomplished the climber, the greater his modesty. Perhaps this is something to do with ambition; when the young climber craves for an objective it becomes all important that he gains it. When he achieves it he goes for the next one; eventually, perhaps, he reaches the conclusion drawn by Doug Scott:

"Ambition feeds on itself and can never be satisfied. You can only let go of it but it is hard to get off the treadmill."

TRAINING

Training is important to help achieve climbing performance. However, climbing action is so diverse, involving very complex muscle interaction, that it is a developing subject of some controversy. I do not intend this to be a comprehensive manual on training. The subject is a book in itself, but I shall highlight some important general points which should be remembered by those intending to train specifically to improve their climbing.

Firstly, let's examine some primary components of performance that are required in climbing. Every climber needs flexibility and suppleness, possibly most of all in technical rock climbing and less so, although they are still important, in ice climbing. Good balance, too, is highly desirable. Specific strength, power and acceleration are absolutely essential to the climber, particularly for the high-performance rock climber, but also strength of arm and leg is vital for the ice climber to wield the tools of his trade. Arguably the most important quality of all is stamina, i.e. the ability to keep going and link moves and protection placement without needing to stop and rest. Admittedly, climbing skill and the minimal use of energy are important here, but training can provide these as well as absolute muscular and physical stamina. The benefit of correct training to improve performance is obvious; the selection of specific training is not so obvious. The following training methods and comments are given to form only the basis of training development and are included solely with the intention of setting the novice on the right course.

TRAINING METHODS

Firstly, the importance of warming up and stretching must be understood. Gentle stretching of the muscles is vital to avoid injury, and emphasis must be placed on the word gentle. After stretching, preliminary exercise should be light until the body is warm and ready for action. There are a number of books on stretching and mobility, and these should be referred to. Secondly, training is only worthwhile if it actually improves climbing performance; exercise is rarely ever worthless but some exercises will do absolutely nothing to improve climbing performance. Therefore, correct selection of routine is vital.

CLIMBING WALLS

A well designed climbing wall is an excellent training facility, but thought must be employed to exploit its full potential. Build up slowly the degree of difficulty, and balance the type of problem tackled with the climbing to be undertaken. There are problems and exercises that can be done purely to gain power and strength, but do not forget the stamina side of climbing wall training. In many respects training for stamina on a climbing wall, by circuiting and staying on the wall for set periods of time without resting, can be more important in the real climbing situation than just training to achieve proficiency on set problems.

GYMNASTIC EXERCISE
Lifting one's own weight, for example doing pull-ups on a bar, is probably one of the best ways for a climber to achieve both overall fitness and power. Different grips for different muscles and use of single arm or individual fingers should be part of the routine.

WEIGHT TRAINING
This is very important for extreme performance. It allows isolation and development of particular muscles. All weight exercises should not be overdone but should be worked at in sets of activity, possibly with the last set, when the muscles are thoroughly warmed, taken to the extreme point where no further weight can actually be lifted. It is essential that exercises undertaken are relevant to climbing usage and knowledgeable advice must be sought to work out specific exercises, loading and routines for the individual climber (different body weights obviously require different lifting loads).

Weight training also enables one to monitor and measure physical performance. It is possible to do an hour's training once a week, gradually increasing the weight as strength and fitness are improved, and to reap a distinct and measured increase in muscle performance. There is no guarantee of increasing climbing performance, of course, but it certainly won't do any harm.

RUNNING
Running provides excellent all-round exercise that builds stamina and fitness and improves leg power. It is essential training for the ice climber and mountaineer, although I know hard core rock climbers who will not run because they regard an increase in leg weight (due to muscle development) detrimental to the power-to-weight ratio which is so important in high standard rock climbing.

FLEXIBILITY AND MOBILITY
Already discussed in connection with warming up before other activity, flexibility and mobility are important in themselves to achieve climbing performance. Many climbers find dance practice, "jazz dance" etc to be an extremely helpful and pleasurable way of improving these two climbing requisites. Yoga and other disciplines of mind and body are also important to many climbers.

BALANCE
Some climbers practise walking along suspended ropes, but I'm rather sceptical as to the actual usefulness of this in the climbing situation. It's good fun though!

HUMOUR
In any serious training programme this is essential. There is nothing worse than a boring training period – have a laugh or two.

RESTING AND THE OVERALL TRAINING PROGRAMME
It is very easy to overtrain and to damage the body. It is imperative that adequate rests are taken in the training programme to allow muscle growth, etc. and, of course, a programmed sequence of training must be undertaken. Random activity, resulting in overtraining, can do more harm than good. I can't be specific here, because training, its frequency and intensity, depends on individual fitness.

However, training must be integrated and as an example of the type of integration I put forward the following is a suggested programme for a reasonably fit climber. If a climber is out climbing every weekend, then a reasonable training programme to maintain and improve performance would be, for instance, two nights on the climbing wall, one for power and one for stamina, a night lifting weights and two to three nights running a medium distance, perhaps around four road miles. Many climbers will say this is ridiculous: some may feel that it is far too light and that they weight train twice every non-climbing day, whereas others will feel that the programme is excessively vigorous. Both will be right: there are no standard rules. If your body feels good and performance improves, then that is the right level of training for you. Listen to your body; in many ways it will tell you what is right.

INJURY

Intense training, particularly on climbing walls where it is very easy to let climbing enthusiasm outweigh sensible judgement, can do extreme damage to the body. Points to watch are tendon strain and snapping and pulling joints. The climber is most vulnerable when he is unfit or when he takes training to excess.

It is also a fact that drug-taking enhances training capacity, by artificial stimulation and by lowering the mind's resistance to boredom and pain. Short term climbing performance may be improved but in the long term it is a recipe for crippling injury.

PERSPECTIVE

Let's put climbing training in some perspective. Don Whillans put up rock climbs of technical grade 6b in the 1950s; he was most certainly one of Britain's finest ever Alpinists and Himalayan climbers and I have good reason to believe he never did a day's training in his life! However, there is no doubt that correctly targeted and balanced training can result in an improvement in climbing performance.

DIET

This is a massive and complex subject about which I intend only to make a few general remarks. Basically, you "get out what you put in"! Health, power, strength, energy and, of course, life itself depend on giving the body the right fuel at the right time and in the right amount.

The body needs carbohydrate for energy, protein for power and a certain amount of fat to store carbohydrate energy. It also needs minerals and vitamins to keep healthy. Climbing is so diverse that diet must match the particular type of climbing you intend to undertake. A high standard rock climber, whose power to weight ratio is critical, requires a different diet from the mountain man. The latter needs needs adequate reserves of energy both to climb and generate enough survival heat. That's as far as I'm prepared to go, for an in-depth analysis is yet another book!

However, I would like to add that there are many diets about in the climbing world which, in my opinion, owe more to fashion than to climbing performance. A considered and balanced diet is the most important concept to grasp. It should be sufficient to provide the body with all its requirements, not just those that enhance any particular temporary situation. A vegetarian diet is fine, but it is also fact that it is not the easiet method of getting protein into the body. So, consider this and weigh up the advantages and disadvantages. I believe in the simplest and freshest foods possible and I stay away from chemical injected synthetic foods. On the other hand, whilst on the hill and requiring a quick restoration of blood sugar level, hence energy, I find chocolate bars and the like the best thing for the job.

A most important consideration is the psychological effect of a diet. If you have a particular diet which you are convinced is doing you good, then that's fine; any small shortcomings in the actual diet may well be countered by the positive mental attitude it gives to your climbing. If you think that your controlled diet and systematic training are helping your climbing performance, they will. I don't say this glibly! If you have that degree of bodily control and discipline, you will undoubtedly have the right positive attitude which is essential to climbing performance.

Drink is another subject altogether, but all I will say here is that basically excess alcohol damages and alters body function. Bear in mind, though, that nothing is perfect and anything in moderation will do little harm to the average person!

Carbohydrate diet. This high standard rock climber, who normally counts every calorie, is on holiday!

Carrying sufficient "hill food" when out on the mountains is important as is getting enough fluid intake. Whilst one should travel as lightly as possible the food must be selected with due consideration given to its "food value". Treat dehydrated meals with some caution: their actual "food value" can be inadequate and if not fully hydrated they can cause severe problems. It is important to carry a lightweight water bottle and some take a small plastic tube to suck up water that would not otherwise be accessible.

ETHICS

Historically, the climbing world has always been bound by unwritten rules. There is an agreed code of practice that defines certain do's and don'ts that are intended to make the climbing game fair, in so much as climbers are performing with equal opportunity and "give the mountains a chance". On close inspection it could be said that most "advances in standard" have been achieved by breaking these rules in some way! But how can you break rules that don't actually exist in the form of the written word? To the non-climber it must seem very confusing.

Whilst it really should be open to the individual to climb as he wants, so long as he doesn't damage the rock or spoil other climbers' enjoyment of the sport, in practice certain ethics prevail. These ethics are usually set by the leading climbers of the day and with the advent of modern technology they seem to be rapidly shifting, i. e. there is no comparison between "free" rock climbing of the Jim Birkett/Bill Peascod era, when they ran out there on "sight leads" with no protection, and the "free" bolt protected routes of today, which are a completely different game. However, life moves on and technical difficulty and technology move with it.

But I digress, so I will return to trying to establish what are ethics. Perhaps if I quote what are considered to be two ethical acts in the climbing world it would help define the parameters of this difficult topic.

There is a famous rock climb in the Lake District called Kipling Groove that was led by Arther Dolphin without any mechanical protection. On an early repeat ascent Joe Brown placed a peg for protection; this outraged the Lakeland climbers and very quickly Pete Greenwood, a leading climber of the area, led the route and spat on the peg as he passed it by. His demonstration that the climb could be done without the peg is a famous historical stand for ethics. Likewise, in mountaineering, Don Whillans, attempting the then unclimbed south-west face of Everest, refused to traverse out to the technically easier South Ridge. To do so would probably have meant that he would have reached the summit of Everest and, of course, reaped huge public acclaim by so doing. This was not the route for Don; he was on the much harder SW Face route. That was the nature of the man.

I suppose, then, ethics have something to do with personal pride, which could explain why there is so much argument and controversy over this extremely nebulous subject. Originally, I intended to cover all the latest terminology and detail of the current ethical field, but on due consideration, apart from boring myself to sleep, the whole question of ethics changes so quickly and differs so greatly regionally and internationally that I feel it would be rather futile to do so.

One subject, however, on which I think it prudent to make my feelings known is that of placing expansion bolts in rock. These cause permanent damage to the rock. The great mountaineer, Reinhold Messner, described the use of expansion bolts as the "murder of the impossible" and I fully agree with this statement.

On European cliffs it is usual to protect "free" rock climbs by using expansion bolts. There are some fabulous rock climbs possible, because they are made safe in this fashion and the technical climbing standards are remarkably high. There is little danger in climbing these routes: they are purely technical problems akin to making moves on a boulder or on a climbing wall a few feet from the ground. On most of these routes protected in this way, generally on steep smooth limestone, it is probably true that there is no other form of protection and that these routes would not exist without the use of expansion bolts.

In Britain there is a great tradition of free rock climbing, on a wide variety of rock types, and long leads with little protection. The protection that is used is mainly that of the nut runner which is placed by a climber's guile and skill and is removed without damaging the rock. Runners and protection used in this fashion do not affect any other climber's pleasure.

The European fashion of placing expansion bolts has hit Britain hard, and I think it warrants some reasoned comment. Somewhere between the "murder of the impossible" and the use of bolts on otherwise protectionless limestone there is a place for bolts. In my opinion it can never be on the traditional mountain crags where great leads have been performed in the past and where the challenge of putting up new routes is not only that of technical gymnastic ability but also that of having the courage to lead without protection if necessary or with the skill to place nut runners that can be placed and removed without permanently damaging the rock.

Today's leading climbers must have a responsibility both to the great climbers of the past and to the next generation, a generation which may well spit on today's expansion bolts as it passes them effortlessly by!

Enjoy your climbing!

BIBLIOGRAPHY

Although most of the following selection of books are of a technical reference nature, I have included some which give important general and historical background.

Anderson, B., *Stretching* (Pelham Books).
Barton, B., *A Chance In A Million – Scottish Avalanches* (Scottish Mountaineering Trust).
Birkett, B., *Lakeland's Greatest Pioneers* (Hale).
Birkett, B., *The Hillwalker's Manual* (Oxford Illustrated Press).
Bonington, C., *I Chose To Climb* (Gollancz).
Borthwick, A., *Always A Little Further* (Diadem).
British Mountaineering Council., *Mountain Hypothermia* (B.M.C.).
Brown, J., *The Hard Years* (Penguin).
Chouinard, Y., *Climbing Ice* (Sierra Club).
Clark, C., *Lightweight Expeditions To The Great Ranges* (Alpine Club).
Cleare, J., *Mountains* (Macmillan).
Cliff, P., *Mountain Navigation* (Cordee).
Fawcett, R., *Climbing* (Bell & Hyman).
Gray, D., *Rope Boy* (Gollancz).
Greenbank, A., *Walking, Hiking and Backpacking* (Constable).
Grisogono, V., *Sports Injuries* (John Murray).
Hulse, S., *First Aid For Hillwalkers & Climbers* (Cicerone Press).
Jackson, J., *Safety on Mountains* (British Mountaineering Council).
Langmuir, E., *Mountaincraft and Leadership* (The Scottish Sports Council).
March, B., *Modern Snow and Ice Techniques* (Cicerone Press).
March, B., *Modern Rope Techniques* (Cicerone Press).
McInnes, H., *International Mountain Rescue Handbook* (Constable).
McNeish, C., *The Backpacker's Manual* (Oxford Illustrated Press).
Patey, T., *One Man's Mountains* (Gollancz).
Peascod, B., *Journey After Dawn* (Cicerone Press).
Pedgley, D., *Mountain Weather* (Cicerone Press).
Robbins, R., *Basic Rockcraft* (La Siesta Press).
Sansom, G. S., *Climbing At Wasdale* (Castle Cary Press).
Shepherd, N., *Self Rescue Techniques For Climbers & Instructors* (Adventure Unlimited).
Unsworth, W., *Encyclopedia of Mountaineering* (Penguin).
Unsworth, W. *Everest* (Macmillan).
Walker, K., *Mountain Navigation Techniques* (Constable).
Whillans, D., *Portrait Of A Mountaineer* (Penguin).

INDEX

Italic entries refer to illustrations and captions